MY DISEASE
MY TEACHER

"without inspiration, there's only desperation"

Matteo Charles

BALBOA.
PRESS

A DIVISION OF HAY HOUSE

Balboa Press books may be ordered through booksellers or by contacting:

Balboa Press
A Division of Hay House
1663 Liberty Drive
Bloomington, IN 47403
www.balboapress.com.au
1 (877) 407-4847

Artwork by Glance Graphic Design

Print information available on the last page.

ISBN: 978-1-5043-0092-6 (sc)
ISBN: 978-1-5043-0093-3 (e)

Balboa Press rev. date: 01/08/2016

Contents

This book is dedicated to my parents and brother who have been my saviours. You have been my legs when I couldn't walk and sat by my side when death was knocking on my door.

To my four-legged son Bentley (the bulldog): you have brought such joy to my life, you never cared what I looked like, how much money I had or what car I drove. Yet every day your little bottom seemed about to fall off from the excitement flowing through your body each and every time you saw me—even if it was just an hour ago. Your gentle soul and loving nature kept my spirits strong.

To the higher source: every day as humans we try to steer our lives in a fast-paced direction, thinking we are in control. The most valuable lesson you have taught me is that I am not in control.

You are the only source of energy who can open doors and close them. When you are ready, you will steer us in the direction we need to go and, as much as that may seem hard to accept, only you know when we are ready.

Thank you for showing me the light, guiding me through the darkness, opening my eyes and allowing me to see beyond the physical place we call Earth.

My Disease, My Teacher is loosly based on true events as lived by author Matteo Charles.

From an ambitious teenage entrepreneur conforming to the material world, with an unstoppable mindset and living the fast life, Matteo thought he knew and had it all.

Unexpectedly diagnosed with an incurable disease, Matteo's world was turned upside down and he lost faith in everything he 'thought' he once knew.

Not accepting his diagnosis, Matteo fought denial, aggravation and depression, finding no refuge within the medical industry for this 'thing' that had temporarily taken over his body, Matteo surrendered his soul to the higher source. He stepped back, looked within and his journey of self-help, reconnecting with himself and breaking down everything he once knew began.

Matteo started to rebuild his mind, body and soul. The journey towards self-discovery, inner wisdom and the true purpose of living was Matteo's only mission. What lay ahead were the greatest lessons, discoveries and spiritual guidance that would question all things in the physical world, giving hope to all sufferers and self-help seekers who feel isolated and alone.

Matteo Charles invites you into his world of wealth, glamour and adversity, sharing his secrets about turning his disease and downfall into the highest form of education one can learn.

Some of life's best lessons are learnt at the worst of times.

Chapter 1

The Blank Canvas

You better bring home a brother! I don't want a sister; you better bring home a brother!

Those words catapulted through the room as my mother left for the hospital to give birth to me. My then six-year-old brother made it clear that he did not want my parents to come home with anything but a newborn baby brother to play with and, to his credit, that wish was granted.

At five pounds fourteen ounces (I hear this from my mother every year on my birthday), I made my way into the physical world; a small bundle of fur, tiny body, and a glow that would light up any room (or so I have been told).

My birthday is three days before Christmas, so my delivery was definitely great timing. A summer baby (in Australia), a Christmas baby, a baby that was on the border of two star signs if you believe in horoscopes, and a baby that would test the hands of time in more ways than one.

Through the lens of a parent, a newborn child is viewed with such purity—no imperfections, a pure soul and a representation of elements such as innocence, beauty and peace. Whenever a newborn is present, a smile seems to be the contagious expression on all who come in contact with that little bundle of joy.

Consider an artist creating a new masterpiece on a blank canvas. Perhaps that artist does not know ahead what will be created but a feeling of joy penetrates that artist from within. It cannot be explained; all the artist needs to do is feel and create. After a certain amount of time, with countless colours and brushstrokes, no set rules or guidelines but lots of passion and technique, a masterpiece is created.

I use this metaphor quite frequently in my life today for many reasons. I see life and each day as a blank canvas, a fresh start to creativity and opportunity. We enter this world pure with no flaws, just as a blank canvas is when unpainted. Over time we develop certain traits. Just as an artist applies paints or 'traits' to the canvas, our characteristics, skill sets, career paths and partnerships are formed. I see this, or translate this, as an artist continuously adding colours to the canvas (or 'layers' as I refer to them) while developing the final artwork. In human terms, the final artwork is what and who we are today.

Humans develop layers in many ways, shapes and forms. However, unlike a canvas covered in thick layers of paint, we can not just paint over that canvas in white and start again … or can we?

I think that when children are born there is already in every parents' unconscious mind a pre-planned or desired path they wish their child to follow. More often than not, that plan is altered by the child's own inner ambitions or lack thereof. From a young age, signs are present as to what each child has an interest in. So the original plan starts to shift and not always in the parents' preferred direction.

There is so much going on when raising a child, especially when a parent has more than one infant running around the house. Signs and personal traits of individual adolescents are often overlooked by the parent and not nurtured into the future development of the youngster. This often leads to one of the following two scenarios:

Scenario One

A child demonstrates signs of talents or gifts that are quickly noticed by a parent or perhaps a school teacher. That child is then supported so the adolescent excels in every aspect of their childhood, becoming what they have been prepared for from a young age.

If a child is the eldest and male, he will play and compete in all sports that time permits—elite levels must be achieved quickly! He will adopt the dominant and protector role and feel obliged to care for his younger siblings. He will top all of his classes throughout school, attending extended tutorials to improve and maintain high grades, ultimately resulting in acceptance into the most prestige university through a scholarship program.

Throughout his university years he will maintain high grades in every class, not taking any chance of jeopardising his sporting or business aspirations, resulting in continuous distinctions. Anything less would, of course, not be acceptable. On graduation, his family's dream of an elite sport contract or entrance to a reputable firm will come to fruition, setting up the path to lifelong success.

Perhaps a daughter was the first born, the epitome of daddy's little girl or princess, and a similar unconscious scenario is instantly instilled in the father's mind. She will grow up in cute pigtails wearing pink all day, have undivided love for her parents and especially her father, attend an all girls private school, enrol in ballet at a young age and continue this pattern throughout her primary and high school life.

Once again, she will maintain high grades. Boys will not be an issue for this educated-focused individual, as she is devoted to her studies. She will continue her schooling career maintaining A grades, resulting in her acceptance into the most prestigious medical faculty. She will go on to become a respectable doctor, find and marry her Prince Charming, create a family and live happily ever after.

Scenario Two

A child's attributes or gifts are dismissed, due to his or her talents not being recognised or nurtured. This results in the child feeling unsure of who they are and lacking direction in their life, often questioning their entire existence.

In many cases, unanswered questions lead to a life of pain that could include a cocktail of drug usage and, in extreme cases, suicide. Meaningless relationships, casual sex, violence and continuous career defeats can become a vicious cycle for those seeking a short hit of pleasure in a world of day-to-day pain, stemming from unanswered questions in childhood.

Now if you're a parent reading this, something from scenario one or two may be all too familiar. Whether good or bad, something has yanked on a few buried emotions that didn't want to resurface. Perhaps you are a teenager or someone of any age or status, female or male of any background. I bet something inside right now is feeling a little uneasy; the emotion of pain has resurfaced or a direct smack in the face has put you right back in reality's chair.

We all want what's best for our loved ones, but I think we can agree that life's cards never allow us to have a full house every time. We all possess protective instincts when it comes to family, some more than others. Whether it's our mother, father, son, daughter, sister, niece or nephew, we always want only the best for them.

But what is 'the best'? Is it first place? Is it brand name material objects? Is it happiness? And who are the individuals who decide what's best? Is there a company with a group of people who travel the world, test all of these 'things' and decide what's best for us? And if that's so, how could they possibly get it right when each person is different in so many diverse ways? Why can't we decide what's 'best' for our own lives?

What if someone—perhaps a mother, father, brother, sister, niece, nephew, aunty or uncle—thinks they know what's 'best' for us, when actually they only know what's 'best' for them? Perhaps they are just instilling in our own lives something they missed out on doing, so they are living their overlooked opportunities through us or else just continuing the circle of life the way they were taught.

What if the path a parent paves for their child from day one creates a trail of destruction because of the blinkers that have been placed over their own eyes from the conformed world? From the minute an infant is born into the physical world, everything that is taught to them is just patterns of past family generations. Parents are too caught up in the web of ego and conformity to know any different.

What if daddy's little princess, who was raised to be polite, well-mannered and appropriately dressed, decides to rebel and steer away from life's paved path and turn everything upside down, creating a world of turmoil and pain? Unimaginably, she mixes with the immoral pack at school and is pressured into taking drugs at an early age; she experiments with boys in an extended revenge act against her father who didn't love her or loved her too much. She enters destructive and abusive relationships that increase her drug usage, which ultimately leads to her fall into homelessness, prostitution and her eventual agonizing death.

What about the pin-up son on the path to becoming a professional athlete who breaks his leg while away at university? Due to the pressure of becoming a professional sportsman, he decides to speed up his recovery process with illegal pain killers because no-one will ever find out. He then becomes dependent on the drugs and enhances his usage, with addiction being the result. He continues to play with an unhealed leg and, after every game, mental exhaustion takes over his entire being.

After years of being a silent drug user and finally graduating from university, he is not chosen to become a professional athlete as everyone had hoped. So after playing for years on that unhealed broken leg, he overdoses in his rented car in a sleazy motel car park.

Why is it that in life we miss thing*s, we miss the warning signs, we miss the obvious signs? Are we so busy that we are blinded by what's so apparent in our everyday lives? Are we just not interested? Do we not understand the warning signs because there is so much information available at our fingertips today? Or is it that we simply don't want to know or understand, hoping that if we sweep it under the carpet it will simply go away.

I think it's deeper than that. I think it's deeper yet still as simple as it can be. It lies deep within every human because it's one emotion that riddles most of us and causes disease in some way, shape or form. It's an emotion that can overtake our lives. It can control us and, if we aren't careful, it will kill us. Mankind knows it, or should I say mankind recognises it as a word that changes human interaction: that word is **fear.**

Are we prepared for the worst? What is the worst? If we don't know, then how can we be prepared? Are we prepared for our daughter's first date; have we raised her well so that we can be confident in her choice of a partner; will she come home pregnant or will she come home at all? All of these questions stem from fear.

As parents, have we prepared our children with enough life skills to eliminate their fears and conquer the world in their own way? Or have we unconsciously raised our offspring to what we think is 'the best' or 'the best way we knew how', when all along all we have really achieved is concreting our own fears and the fears that were instilled into us from generations before, as the chain was never broken and the circle of fear (not life) continued.

Life isn't perfect. That word 'perfect' places such high demands and pressures on humanity when it has no one true meaning. If there were an authentic, single meaning for the word it would help, because then humanity would at least have a target to aim at.

I think many of us travel on life's path knowing that somewhere along the way, no matter, what something will go wrong. But we hope and pray—to whoever it is you hope and pray to—that nothing will go wrong.

Many of us 'knock on wood', another common saying that's been around for generations. It continues to be used despite it having no real meaning or any proof that knocking on wood will stop any disaster from happening! No matter how much we hope and pray or knock on wood that something doesn't go wrong, more times than not something will. Then when it does, we are forced to face that second nasty emotion which leads to physical implications and that is **pain**.

Pain is another word that humanity has given a negative meaning to, and it has become stronger and stronger over time. Sure, if you fall off your bike and graze your knee and have to get six stiches to stop the bleeding that is painful, right? It will hurt maybe for a week or two, then the stitches are removed and you never think of that pain again. If you are lucky, you are left with a nice scar that you can use to break the ice when meeting someone for the first time!

Whether we choose to ignore it, deal with it, or try to avoid it, pain enters everyone's life at some stage in some form or another. But what if pain was fun, a form of learning? Imagine you are riding along the footpath on a new bicycle you just bought yesterday. You haven't ridden for years but you know what you are doing so you take it down to your local park. You jump on, it's great that no-one is around and the path is empty. Your speed starts to increase, you gain confidence, your speed increases further and you start to manoeuvre side to side. What a great feeling! You notice a small ledge coming up, your confidence is at its highest as is your speed, you approach the ledge squat down and lift off, stand up and, before you know it, you are airborne and about to clear the ledge when bang! You land in the worst possible way, throwing yourself off the bike, causing you to gash your leg resulting in six stiches.

Now this incident causes you temporary pain, right? But the pain isn't deep enough to be so traumatic it never allows you to ride again. In fact, it actually teaches you a very valuable lesson. Learn to ride before you can jump, or crawl before you can walk as the saying goes.

So what if pain was always delivered at the same level, meaning temporary until the wound was healed and the stitches were removed. Could we take life by the horns with so much more confidence? And could we learn and be taught so much from our pain? Instead of viewing the discomfort as something that is harming us, could we see it as something that is teaching us a valuable lesson from the 'University of Life'?

Life isn't easy, but it can be easier if we pay attention and don't submit to conformism but rather listen to the one source that continues to teach us in the most non-traditional way. And that is **life**.

I'm sure you have heard this expression many times: *Life is what you make of it.* But you can only make of it what you already know, meaning what you have been taught by your elders. If your elders have not been taught by life themselves, you will not gain these insights from them.

Humans experience the same things in different ways, resulting in so many outcomes for us without necessarily learning from those experiences. Our choices and emotion-driven reactions can alter our entire existence. Over time and despite their intelligence, humans choose to ignore many things and continue the same patterns, resulting in heartache, turmoil and disease.

~~~~~~

Throughout this book, I will illustrate my life, and how certain decisions have resulted in things that I am certain my parents never thought would ever happen, nor did I.

I want to show you how to listen to that little voice inside you and see signs as signs and not coincidences. I want to help you, no matter what level of life you are at, to find your passion. It's there; it's just asleep right now if you haven't found it or it hasn't found you yet.

I want to show you that when things are rough—and they will get rough—it's for a reason. In times of pain, you may not see the particular reason or lesson, for emotion will overtake your body without your permission. But I will provide you with the tools to take hold and rid yourself of emotional reaction and, in turn, only act from knowing.

Things are not meant to be easy. If they were, lessons wouldn't be learnt. We would not appreciate things if they were easy; how do you know what pleasure is, if you don't know what pain feels like?

Think about a material item you have always wanted and finally received, or think about something you want right now that seems to be unattainable due to its high value. The real reason the item becomes more valuable to you once it's obtained is not because it's a brand name and of high value. Sure, it will feed your ego. But the real reason is because of what it took to place you in the position of being able to purchase this 'thing' that only a few months ago seemed so far out of your reach.

The process towards obtainment teaches you patience (knowing that things just don't come straight away), finance (how to save for something or rearrange your position in life to be able to afford the finer things in life) and lastly maintenance (the upkeep of the product, ensuring its lifespan to be the longest possible with the correct care in place, just like our bodies).

In life we need to face our fears and we can use that to enhance our growth in so many ways. We need to be able to make wrong decisions, so we learn from them and mature.

So start making mistakes. Not literally for the sake of it but to allow life to guide you. Keep an open mind, but not so open that you take in things that have no way of enhancing your life.

Allow the important elements to stand out, and they will. You will know what's important, who is needed and what is needed at the right time, ultimately leading you to live your true purpose.

Experiment, ask questions, don't stop learning, and be awake. Our eyes and ears are open every day, yet many of us seem to be blinded by life's distractions and have become deaf to nature's glory.

Open your heart to the heavens, spread your wings and be you; not the 'you' your parents, friends or society want you to be. Be the you that allows your soul to jump out of bed each morning with excitement about living.

Become the you that allows a glow to resonate from your soul, illuminating a sense of calmness and happiness within your day's activities and that is contagious to every being, just like the flu. But this is the best flu one can catch, because the only drug needed is life and that is the cause and the cure; nothing more, nothing less; purity at its rawest form. Now that's living!

Chapter 2

The First Brush Stroke

Just go Mum. I'll be fine; go home.

My brother is six years older than I am, so he got to experience most things first. Those were his famous words on the first day of kindergarten. Mum and I walked him to school daily and each morning he couldn't wait to get there. Mum tells us that he was ready to learn, meet new people and begin his life as a student.

It's funny because if you were to meet him today, he is very similar: an intelligent businessman, not afraid to take the bull by the horns and get in the ring if need be. He loves to network and is continuously learning, so his personality and traits have remained constant throughout his life.

For some people like my brother, the first brush stroke comes naturally. Some see life as an artist, starting each day as though it were their new blank canvas. They view life as a blank canvas, knowing exactly what they want out of their existence (their final art work) and they begin to paint their path or masterpiece of life from a tender age.

This type of artist or person is similar in character to my brother. Already have a confidence within, they see the canvas and instantly a colour palette appears combined with a clear vision and they begin to create.

To others, who I have found to be the majority, the first brush stroke doesn't come so naturally. Well, not at the beginning anyway and I fell into this category. As a child I was quite reserved, very introverted and didn't like to be centre of attention unless around my family or friends. It was like I had a split personality.

Mum tells the story of my first day at school. I wouldn't stop crying for hours before leaving home; I didn't want to go. I attended the same school as my brother, so in theory my insecurities and anxiety should not have been so high, given that he was only a few classrooms away.

My mother remembers my first day. She remembers that I made myself sick, kept vomiting, and she had to walk me to the classroom while all the other children were sitting patiently, waiting for this insanely loud and emotional child who wouldn't let his mum go. to Finally, my mother put on her brave hat. While she was emotional about seeing her son so upset, she built up the courage and walked away, listening to my screams. My mother recently told me she didn't leave the school for at least two hours each morning for the first month, wanting to ensure I was okay.

Now it's strange that I felt so insecure, scared and threatened about starting school, when my upbringing was very similar to someone who couldn't wait to enhance his learning capabilities daily, meet new people and give anything a go.

Did something happen in my early childhood that I didn't know about to entrench insecurity within, without me knowing. I was an infant, how could I know? I didn't know what insecurities were, so how could I crave for my mother not to leave me when it was just school? I knew she would return to pick me up, because I observed the process happen with my older brother. So why was I so affected by this simple, normal human experience?

Was it a deeper problem; was it not of this world? All too often, we see through our physical eyes something that disturbs us as humans; we don't know why it disturbs us, but it does. A screaming child, a drug addict, a homeless person, someone who is wealthier than us—it affects us and plays on our emotions, causing us to conduct the worst form of human interaction today: **stereotyping**.

When we come into contact with others, the first thing we do (no matter how much time we have before we start communicating with words) is judge: *What is she wearing? Look at their teeth! Oh, as if you would be driving that! They must have money!*

Then bang! Reality slaps you right in the face and you float back to earth, instantly sparking conversation with that person you were so quick to judge, only to find out you were actually immoral with your judgmental thoughts. This is someone you could see yourself being friends with or even more.

Just as when I was that screaming child, not wanting to be left alone or ripped from his mother's arms, I bet many mothers in the playground before the bell rang for school each day would have stared at my mother thinking: *What is wrong with that child? I'm glad he is not mine!*

You see, every emotion is invisible yet is born, created, instilled from somewhere. It may be of this world, it may be from past lives we have lived, it may be from something we picked up on our own. But it had to be created from somewhere.

Understanding this can change the negativity that this planet has instilled in many of us, such as anger that is unnecessary. I'm not suggesting that you go around and hug everyone saying: *Hey, it's all good and life is awesome!* because for many it's not. And most likely, you would receive a punch in the face or worse.

But what if we removed our everyday glasses and looked at life (say) like a superhero? What if we could really see the core of someone else's problems, something they could not see within themselves or did not want to see within themselves, due to the amount of emotional pain they were suffering? Perhaps we could then help them and steer them away from a vicious life of pain and turmoil.

Don't judge a mother whose child is screaming, as the infant may simply be hungry. Maybe that mother is a single parent with four other children to provide for, fighting to keep a roof over their heads and barely keeping their stomachs full. But I guess she won't be wearing a T-shirt that says all of this, so how could we possibly know?

What if today you could become a better person … you could help others and eliminate pain, not only from your life but from everyone you come into contact with … would you do it? Think about it: a world with no famine, no war, no homelessness, just happiness, one big rainbow of joy. Would you spread the love?

Well you can, and it all starts with the first brushstroke. Doing or starting something for the first time is always daunting, whether your first day at school, a job interview, driving lesson, first date or even your first kiss. It's all new so it's scary; sometimes exciting scary but most of the time it just scares the living daylights out of you.

A job interview is a common cause for fear in society today. Say it's a position you really desire for a reputable company; you possess all of the key characteristics and skill set to will fill the position; there's nothing that can affect your chances of gaining employment; you have got this.

You are wearing your new suit, perhaps new high heels, your hair is working out perfectly today, no frizz. Oh wow, no traffic on the way in and you've even left with enough time to compensate for traffic. Law of attraction, nothing can go wrong now.

You arrive at your destination an hour prior to your interview. You spot a cafe nearby and decide you are going to enjoy a nice coffee to enhance the positive energy around you before the interview. 'One large skim cappuccino please' you order.

You casually make your way over to a free table that's all of a sudden became available in this busy cafe. You can't believe your luck today and, to top it off, it's situated right near a window with sunlight shining right on it, like the angels were inviting you to sit with them. You hop and sing over to that table, sit down and close your eyes and just take a moment to embrace the sun and all the good vibes the morning has brought about. You're ready to take on the world or, in this case, your interview.

You slowly float back to earth as the waiter heads towards you with your hot beverage. You smile and get ready to greet him when, all of a sudden, it's like the world turns into slow motion. The waiter trips only a metre away from you, the large coffee flies through the air, the chocolate supported by the silky smooth froth is now airborne with the hot milk in the rear and—splat!—lands all over your new clothes.

In most cases not a big deal, right? These things happen. But in this case, you are about to walk into the interview of your life with a massive coffee stain on your new attire.

Instantly, a million thoughts and emotions race through you mind: *I can't believe this is happening to me right now! Stupid waiter! Where's the bathroom?* All of these questions race through your mind; you're not even worried about the third degree burns your physical body is experiencing. All you can think about is what the interviewer will think as you walk into the interview looking like you had just had a fight with the waiter downstairs and the waiter had won!

Now if we stop and think for a moment, I am sure a similar situation has happened to you or to someone you know. The outcome usually stems from the false reality of what I call 'thinking other people's thoughts'. What do I mean by this? Well, allow me to explain.

When we judge others, we are really thinking other people's thoughts: *What is she wearing? What will they say? What will they think?* Our mind actually starts to develop inferior, meaningless conversations that actually are fake and non-existent. Why are they fake? Because they are all started and created by you, your mind and your ego.

You see, judging someone's screaming child or worrying about what someone will say about the stain on your clothes can be the start of the first brushstroke to disaster. The ultimate result is not creating a masterpiece within every situation but actually needing to start with a new piece of canvas for each and every part of your day, resulting in multiple unfinished pieces or artwork or baggage left as 'things' lying around your physical or spiritual house.

Now this is a hard concept to grasp, especially for the conformed, emotional, overreactive species we have become. Imagine we eradicated stereotypes and negative thoughts promoted by media and advertising, as though they were deadly diseases and we needed to find a cure.

Well, I hate to be the bearer of reality but negativity, judging others and not being you are all diseases. I don't think we could place them under the same banner as the popular diseases often spoken about today. But in my opinion, they are just as deadly as your mainstream money making councils or raising millions to conduct medical research to find cures then, once discovered, keeping the discoveries from mainstream people.

You might think that I'm going a little overboard labelling negativity as a disease. But, as many who are close to me know, everything I say and do is for a reason. I would not write such words if I could not back up my theory. Allow me to paint a picture ...

The first brushstroke in every situation is so important. It sets up a stepping-stone to your next stroke, until you reveal your final piece. If you aren't aware of your first stroke—where it happens, when it needs to happen and how to execute it with precision and emotional control—you are only setting yourself up to paint from an empty can.

Let's revert back to the coffee shop situation. We are at the point where the waiter has spilt hot coffee all over you. Now the emotionally-driven individual will jump up in a rage, kicking, screaming and finger pointing. In some extreme situations, violence will be the end result.

All of these negative impulse reactions have stemmed from the 'fight' element within the fight or flight mode, as your appearance has been tampered with, and the way you will be viewed or 'judged' in your interview won't be favourable. Instantly, your first brushstroke (your appearance) is now the dullest colour on your palette.

But what if you could instantly eradicate all of the dull colours on your palette and only work with the brightest colours every day of your life? Well, you can and it's simple. I will illustrate how, because if you do not learn how to apply the first brushstroke with precision in almost every situation, you will either run out of paint or be dissatisfied with the end result you create.

Now we can't control other people's emotions, thoughts and reactions. I wouldn't really want to, even if I could. I would be too tired fixing other people's problems, instead of continuously growing myself.

But while we may not be able to control other people's actions, we can control our own. This in turn has an effect on others, resulting in an altered way of thinking, from whoever comes into contact with you. You will be an indirect teacher, when the whole time you are well aware of the lesson you are about to illustrate to those you are about to come into contact with.

Take the coffee shop/interview situation. Sure, a negative result can come from this, but what good would it do? In reality, it will kill every chance you ever had of gaining employment with your dream company, as the interviewer will immediately feel the negative emotion or wall you have put up as soon as you enter the room. Have you ever heard the expression: *You can cut the tension in this room with a knife?* Well, the knife would need to be replaced by a samurai sword from the amount of anger and negativity that will project from your soul as you enter the interview room.

Don't allow the emotion to kick in or take over your body; be conscious of what you do. It is very hard and takes practice. Just as going to the gym once does not gain you an instant sixpack, it takes hard work and dedication, so train your mind at home first.

Think of your lifestyle today ... there must be one or more situations that really test your emotional rollercoaster. Pick one of the worst, a situation or person who really puts you over the edge, and place yourself in that situation daily if you can.

It's best to place yourself in a situation that's close to home and doesn't put you in a position of losing too much, such as your dream job. Continue to do this with the intent of learning to control and master your emotions, until you feel no negative attachment to that situation any more. Don't place a time limit and don't let anyone know what you are doing. Allow yourself to become your own teacher without outside influence. Each time you feel rage, breathe in and out and continue to do so in that current situation until the rage has eased.

By becoming your own teacher and getting involved in a personally-managed situation, you will become aware of your emotions and how you handle them. This will instantly provide you with data about how your emotional clock dictates your life, allowing a shift to happen when needed.

Once you have mastered your first emotional test of controlling your emotions in a reactive situation and are then faced with a similar situation as sitting in a coffee shop with coffee all over you prior to the most important meeting of your life, you will find that the interview will actually pan out better than expected and you will turn the situation into a laughable, lighthearted joke.

Walking into the interview you could say: *Hi, my name is Matt. Before we commence formalities, I do have a coffee stain on my shirt. But it's okay because the waiter was having a bad day. Instead of yelling at him when he spilt my coffee all over me as I was about to walk into my dream job interview I stopped, looked at him and said, 'It's okay bud, when I get this job I will make sure I come back every morning to buy a coffee from you. Now where's the mop? I will help you clean up, so no-one slips and hurts themselves.'*

Imagine saying that to a panel of people who have their interview boss hats on, ready to attack you with a million and one questions. You would have just broken down every wall they have placed in front of themselves to protect their company with the greatest most confident lighthearted icebreaker there is.

A day later you receive a call back, confirming you have been successful in gaining the position. Now you didn't land the job because you were better looking, more intelligent, and especially because of what you were wearing. Would you like to know why you were successful in gaining the position?

I mentioned earlier that the first brushstroke is most important. Well in this case, the first brushstroke (how you presented yourself to the panel) was unlike anyone they had ever witnessed. You walked in with an air of confidence, even though you looked like you had been through a coffee car wash.

You made a joke of the situation and demonstrated how you are an out of the box, quick-thinking, troubleshooting individual. And that's exactly what they were looking for to fill the position, all stemming from a situation that could have altered the path to your entire life, if you were not prepared mentally.

Obviously as a child it may be quite hard to mentally prepare for such a situation, as all you are really concerned about is what crayon you will use to draw all over the kitchen, bathroom and bedroom walls. But as adults leading the children of the world, we do have the option to learn, develop and control our emotionally-driven reactions and the first brushstroke, perhaps not in our own lives, but indirectly to help others.

You see, when I was the screaming child in a classroom not wanting to let his mother go, my mother was feeling the pressure of her child yelling and hurting emotionally, as any parent would. I am confident that in the back of her mind lay a small amount of embarrassment about how she would be viewed through the eyes of the school and other parents.

My mother wasn't a bad parent; she knew that, I knew that. But here is the kicker to the outside world. At first glance, it might have seemed as though she was. Why would I have been screaming like I was being murdered? To the untrained mind—the judgemental, stereotypical individual—that's exactly how she would have been viewed.

What if a teacher or an overreactive parent viewed the situation through their blurry vision goggles and took it one step further and contacted some sort of child protection authority anonymously, to assess our situation? My mother would have been devastated to see someone come to her home, a home she kept clean each and every day, food always on the table, a safe roof over our heads and a loving father who provided for us every day.

Imagine the health implications, stress, depression and unanswered questions, with my mother becoming a silent sufferer, all from a situation created by someone who had not learnt how to control their inner, emotional, reactive system.

Now let's reverse the situation. We are back at my first day of school. I am screaming, my mother is walking away but instead of the other mothers overreacting, one approaches her and gently says: *It's okay; my little girl was like your boy the first day I dropped her off. A few mothers are going out for a coffee now close by the school. We would love for you to join us and, if your son needs you, you will only be five minutes away.*

What a change of course one's life would take! Instantly, a sea of calm would resonate as all of the 'fake thoughts' that the other mothers are thinking are quickly eradicated, due to the relatable mother who had just approached my mother to ease her pain.

Did it work? Of course, as being nice and helping others, not judging them, comes at no cost. But we must remember when we choose (and yes, that's right, we do choose whether it's unconscious or conscious) we are choosing to be in a negative or positive state of mind. The implications are not only felt in our own lives but the reciprocators' lives also and can have a very dangerous ripple effect.

As we can never understand the extent or depth of someone's internal pain, all it may take is a small, harmless (well, harmless to you) insult or joke that was intended for a bit of fun. But its delivery time couldn't be worse and the result can lead to disease and, if continued, a life of pain and early death.

So from this point on, let's not make instant decisions to judge, insult or even joke with intent to harm, as we have not taken the time to learn about someone, where their first brushstroke has started and where they intend to finish.

Who knows? You may even save someone's life with the time you have taken to help or listen. I know that if it wasn't for the lady who took the time to relate to my mother and ask her to join her for a coffee on my first day of school, who knows what impact it might have had on her and the ripple effect throughout my entire life.

The funny thing is that each and every day I was at school, so my mother tells me, she would have coffee with the same group of mothers. And each day she would return to pick me up, she would feel a sense of calm knowing she wasn't being judged. It was as though I could sense that as a boy, so day by day it became easier to leave me. Eventually I would walk to school with my brother, not needing her by my side at all.

Years later, I would enter high school with a best friend who was female, like a sister. I never knew why I felt a connection to her but I gravitated to her in my early years and somehow she would be in my class each and every year of primary school. She was the daughter of the lady who approached my mother many years ago to join her for a coffee. We never learnt of this story until we entered high school. We didn't think much of it then but, as I reminisce, I see now it was the higher source working in the way things needed to happen.

Chapter 3

Adding Colour

Matt, hurry up! We are going to be late; I will go without you!

Unlike primary school, on my first day of high school I wasn't screaming and didn't need my mum to walk me to my classroom, although I still felt quite anxious every day for some reason.

I would enter this chapter of my life, well the first year anyway, with my brother in his final year at the same high school and me in my first. Each morning would begin with me sleeping in and him screaming at me because he liked to arrive at school early, check out the scene and socialise. I liked to show up just as the bell rang for class, not a minute more not a minute less, just on time.

I wasn't big in size. I was a pipsqueak really, short, skinny, of European descent, with one of those horrible puberty moustaches growing by the second year of high school which my dad wouldn't allow me to shave, as I was too young.

In my later years I was relatively popular in high school. But in my first year I was just working everything and everyone out, plus my brother was attending the same school, so I didn't want to splash too much paint on his canvas. I wanted to lay low and be a neutral colour, if you will.

Mainly older students bullied me quite a lot in my first year but never anyone from my grade. The funny thing was that I didn't see myself as an easy target or perhaps that was the problem. I was unconsciously seeing myself as a target, which in turn made me one.

I was bullied for eight months of the first year by the same person. For every roll call, I remember that our class was combined with three older grades. The bully was two years older than I was and, for some reason, each roll call we had to have a book to read or we would get into trouble. Each day he would walk in, take my book, grab me by the neck, squeeze and say: 'If you tell anyone you're dead!'

Now this guy wasn't huge in stature but the threat and look in his eyes and the firm grip every day on my neck was enough to instil fear in me. What made it worse was that each day after stealing my book he would scream out loud to the teacher that I didn't have anything to read, which would see me on detention at lunch, picking up rubbish in the playground as punishment.

I never told my parents about the bully. I was too scared; the fear was too strong to voice my concern. But I couldn't hide it from my brother as he attended the same school, and for two days each week the seniors would have lunch with the juniors. So it was only a matter of time before my brother saw me involuntarily picking up other people's rubbish.

I was good at hiding things. I would usually go and pick up rubbish in the oval on shared lunch days, as I knew my brother wouldn't hang out in that area of the school. But one day a close friend of my brother witnessed me picking up papers and told him.

That night he came into my room and asked why I was picking up rubbish at school. I broke down, shaking uncontrollably. I think it was a combination of fear and the stress of not being able to tell anyone about the bully that I had to face every morning at 10.40am—especially my brother, as we were quite close.

The next day I went to school as normal. I had packed two books, prepared for my shakedown but, to be honest, I would never have brought out my second book, from fear that the bully would snatch that from me as well and probably belt me for being smarter than he.

I walked into roll call and sat head down in my usual seat. I would always wear high top jackets, so when his hand wrapped around my neck it wouldn't hurt as much and wouldn't leave a bruise. (This type of forward thinking would serve a greater purpose in my later years.)

There he was, walking into the room straight towards me. I had closed my book ready to hand to him; he was a metre away when our eyes met and then bang! He walked straight past me, didn't even look at me and my book was still in front of me. I was in shock; I was so shocked I almost grabbed myself by the neck and handed the book straight to him.

Given that this abuse had happened each and every day, five days a week for about eight months straight, for it to stop felt wrong. As silly as that may sound, it become a part of my daily routine and it felt weird.

Roll call that day was probably the longest twenty minutes of my life. When that bell rang I grabbed my bag, my book and ran out. I glanced at the teacher on the way out with a look that said: 'I won't be picking up any rubbish today, thank you!'

That day we had shared lunch with the seniors and I had to find my brother. I knew where he hung out every day: top quad, left hand side, set of long aluminium seats, third seat down. That was his spot with his five closest friends. I ran to him with the biggest smile on my face, calling his name. As I approached, I wanted to hug him. I loomed closer and it was like the whole world was put on pause except for him and me. Our eyes met and for a minute we were communicating without words.

I think that was my first indirect spiritual experience but I didn't realise it at the time. I was too young, not open to that realm. But looking back, I see how the workings of the greater source were in play.

As I approached my brother he gave me a look, a look as though he were saying telepathically: 'Just be happy; don't thank me, don't question how, just be happy and enjoy your life. You're safe now, so never speak of it again.'

Then the world continued as normal again, with everyone moving as if nothing had happened. As I approached my brother and his friends, we gave a casual 'Hey!' and I moved on and regrouped with my cluster of friends at the other end of the playground.

To be honest, to this day we have never spoken about the incident. I know my brother did something, either directly or indirectly, to eliminate that pain from my everyday life. I don't think he physically hurt the bully, as that's not who my brother is. Also, I would see the bully each day in roll call and he wasn't battered or bruised. All I needed to know was that the rest of my high school days would be free of pain.

When adding colour to a painting, if the colour palette is off it can make even the most elegant of illustrations look as though an infant has scribbled without direction and intent. But when thought through with precision, every colour added to a painting allows that painting to connect and jump off the canvas to all eyes viewing it.

High school may not be the most important element to a human's overall living capabilities, but I like to describe high school as the important layers added to a canvas, preparing it for a high-end gallery for sale, allowing the masterpiece to speak without words to prospective buyers. You are the masterpiece, your education is the layers, and your overall form of employment or business are your buyers.

Although I believe life's important lessons cannot be learnt in any conformed environment and character can only be formed through adversity, high school is a great playground to indirectly begin your networking skills, communication skills and of course, liaising with the opposite sex, partly preparing you for life's journey.

After my first year of being tucked away in a shell due to one bully, the remainder of my high school years were quite different. I became the 'it' kid, the funny guy, the class clown. By this time, my brother had left school and entered the workforce so I was all on my own. But that didn't matter, I had made friends with every group you could think of—the sporty kids, the nerds, the gangsters. You name it, I was a part of it and I was loving it.

Daily there were multiple high fives and laughs from my jokes. Even teachers would enjoy a giggle from my charisma. Such confidence would resonate and beam out of me. The bully was still around, still in the same roll class, but each day I would notice dark bags under his eyes. He wouldn't be at school most days and, when he attended, it was as though he was on another planet and would often talk to himself.

The bully left school a year before his graduation. I found out later in life that he was actually expelled, as he had become highly addicted to drugs and was becoming violent towards teachers. Only a few years later, I found out from school friends that the bully had died from a drug overdose. I was quite disturbed by this news even though he used to hurt me each day. It is only when I heard the news of his passing that I took time to wonder how and what had led him down that path of anger and destruction, ultimately leading to an early death.

As I grew older, I would extend my thoughts deeper and always cast back to the bully. I would wonder again what first brushstrokes he must have taken to lead him to leave this Earth at such a young age. Was his bullying a way of indirectly reaching out to me, not knowing how to

27

illustrate to the world that he was hurting within and that the only way to feel some sort of release, pain or pleasure was to hurt others?

You would think teachers would have picked up on his issues, given that his patterns of violence gradually increased over time and his appearance was far from healthy. How could something so obvious slip through the system? Who was he hanging around with? Did he surround himself with similar individuals or people who persuaded him to live a dark life?

For me, the first year of high school wasn't so pleasant but after that I found my own place. I wasn't a highly intelligent individual; the areas and subjects I excelled in were English and Art but all other subjects I would just pass.

Art was my saviour, my outlet and my soul speaking to the world. Ever since I had been that crying, screaming child in kindergarten, my mother would say that the only sea of calm that would breeze into my life was art. I would sit for hours and scribble, colour and draw. High school was a great place to harness that energy. I always attended extra classes, stayed back to finish certain pieces and my work was always a stand-out from other students. Every piece I created really made people stop and stare and spark conversation. I didn't realise the power that I was holding in the palm of my hand; I would be slapped in the face by it in my later years.

Apart from Art, English was another subject that captured my soul's attention. It was another class where I would be quiet, pay attention and not be cracking jokes or pranking other students leading to the usual *Matt that's it, get out!* outburst from my teachers, resulting in me walking out to a stream of laughter and applause from other students.

I really don't know why I felt the need to be centre of attention. Maybe I unconsciously felt I needed to be heard, needed to be noticed, prove some sort of a point. Perhaps it stemmed from almost a year of being tucked away in my shell, frightened by a bully. It's funny that all the times I would get kicked out of class there was something in the back of my mind telling me that what I was doing wasn't right; that being loud and noticed wasn't something I should be doing; that it was wiser to be quiet and keep to myself. But who was I to listen to the little voice inside? I was a high school student and I wanted to be cool; well, what I thought was the image of cool at that time.

I attended high school over ten years ago. Back then, we didn't have all of the social media outlets at our fingertips, social pressure was nowhere near what it is today. I guess life was easier, less cramped and I don't mean person-to-person ratio—I mean information.

Masses of unnecessary information weren't crammed down our throats everywhere we looked. Sure, there was advertising on bus shelters, in magazines, but we didn't pay attention. We were busy doing our own thing, going to friends' houses, playing outside—yes playing outside—not flicking things on a screen meaninglessly 24/7 depicting we are ever so busy to others, when we are just flicking through our phone contacts waiting for some one to call so we look important, or reading opened emails over and over to see if we have missed anything from the last time we read it only three minutes ago.

Having so many distractions in high school today can be dangerous. It doesn't allow you to be yourself, you become someone controlled by the outside conformed world, resulting in you becoming someone or something of the system. But here's the kicker … there are so many outlets today telling us to never give up, follow our dreams, live with passion and purpose, and work in our dream job. We all know that when you work within your passion, work becomes play, right?

But how can we become who we are when we don't have the time in our early years (meaning high school) to develop our layers and colours and discover the most important element of our lives? Our passion, our dreams, and most importantly, our God-given talents.

As I mentioned, I excelled in Art and English. However the important subjects—well, what I thought to be the important subjects because those were the ones my elders stressed that I needed to excel in—I didn't do well in at all. I would know just enough to pass, then I would revert back to my passions. But Art and English are not favourable subjects to the outside world. I would constantly be told: *You can't make money from art and writing, so just do them as a hobby.*

That would both confuse and anger me. I was confused because if these subjects were something you 'couldn't earn a living from' why teach them? Why not only teach what we can earn a living from; makes sense, right? And it would anger me when I thought about why I couldn't earn my living from art and writing. I studied history I knew that both subjects had been practised from the stone ages, so why were my elders so convinced that these two subjects were so frowned upon as professions? This instilled a negativity towards the only two areas in life I felt at ease with.

You see, being creative or not following the norm in life scares people, because many are afraid to follow their own dreams. They have been conformed to become (say) a doctor as it is a reputable field to be in; and it's a great feeling to introduce your son or daughter and say they are a doctor. For some, the medical fields are their calling; they may feel the need to heal the world and becoming a doctor is their way of doing so. Others may feel the need to be around children, so they go on to become teachers.

But it's the creative ones who often find themselves in the biggest cloud of confusion. Most of the time creative people seem scattered and withdrawn. But inside their minds, the wheels of creation, conception and design are working silently. They say the quietest mouths have the loudest minds.

I had no idea what I wanted to be when I left school. I always wanted to be in animation, as drawing and illustration were my true passions.

However I never voiced my interest, as it had been drummed into my head that I could not earn a living from my art.

Towards my later years in high school, I found myself becoming bored and irritated. Besides art and writing nothing else stimulated my senses. I would go home daily and continue to sketch or write, always neglecting my homework. My parents would receive my grades via the post and noticed I wasn't doing too well.

I distinctly remember one day when my father returned home from work. He would return each day from work at 3.45pm so my mother would flick the kettle on at 3.40pm to have his daily tea ready when he walked through the door.

Now my father is far from being an aggressive person; to be honest, to this day he is the only person that I know who would live ego free. He is and always has been about his family; he has worked hard his entire life and never questions anything. He does what he has to do to provide for his family, and my brother and I never went without.

So with such a loving family at home, there would be no reason for me to feel insecure, anxious and a little on edge ever, right? Well again in theory that would be the right outcome, but in life I have found (and this would be thrown in my face medically in my later years) that practice and theory don't always match. And I felt that this particular day wasn't going to end with a positive outcome.

I was sitting in my room sketching as per usual. I was in the zone. I remember I was sketching a portrait; portraits were a weak area in my art life, so I wanted to enhance my skills. A black and white charcoal illustration; I remember at one point taking a step back and thinking, *You've got this, Matt.*

I heard my father walk in. I would usually walk out to greet him but today I was in my own world sketching and nothing would take me out of the master's creative chair. Boy, was I wrong!

It's funny how in life certain things stand out when they are in among a cluster of things. You may be reading a book and, on a particular page, there's two words that just beam out at you as though they were highlighted and in bold italic underlined capital letters. Then you step back and realise you needed that little deposit from the angels above to make that next move in life positive or negative, but it needed to be noticed.

This day, my deposit from the angels was the envelope opening as my father sat down to drink his tea. It was as though I could hear a thousand trees falling in the forest when he opened my report card that day.

'Mattttt, get in here!!' I knew instantly the results weren't good. I quickly jumped up and, as I approached my closed door to open it and face the music, I realised my hands were black, covered in charcoal from the portrait I was entrenched in only a minute ago. I didn't know what to do. If I opened the door, I knew I would leave black marks all over it and my father would most likely belt me for that. At the same time, if I didn't get out there quickly enough he would belt me for taking too long. 'Mattttttt, get out here now!!' he screamed again.

My body was trembling; fear had entered my life again. I didn't know what to do. Perfectly timed, my mother opened the door to see me standing there with a look of fear on my face and my hands held above my chest, as though I was meditating standing up. She made her way to the bathroom, opened the door and turned on the tap saying, 'Wash your hands'.

By this time my mother had gone and told my father I was getting cleaned up. I knew this wasn't going to be good, so I think I washed my hands for at least ten minutes, trying to think of my getaway answer for why I wasn't doing so well at school. I always had an answer; good, bad or in-between I could always string something together. But today, all that was going through my mind was … nothing. I drew a blank, so I just continued to wash my hands. 'What are you washing, your entire body? Get out here'! Dad yelled.

I had extended the handwashing process enough. Dad was getting irritated, so it was time to face the music. I slowly walked towards him; he was sitting in the lounge room with my mother beside him. I sat directly opposite him on a little footstool. 'What's this crap?' I didn't know how to reply.

Dad spent the next ten minutes, which felt like an hour, yelling and individually going through each subject and discussing where and why I was failing. I didn't know what was worse, my father yelling at me (as it was rare to hear his voice at that level) or him painting a picture of reality (in my case, how much I was a failure at school).

Once my father's rant had finished I was speechless. It ended with him saying, 'Get out my sight!' So I did, back to my room, headphones on continuing with my sketch.

Two hours later it was dinnertime; I wasn't hungry but we ate as a family. By this time my brother was home from work and had been informed about my disappointing report card. Now my brother, despite enjoying high school, had decided to enter the workforce early at the age of sixteen. He'd landed an apprenticeship in the printing industry at a reputable firm where my grandfather had worked. My brother loved it; he was earning an income, was buying his own things and on his way to creating a greater purpose in his life.

Dinner was silent that night. There was mainly conversation between my parents and my brother about his work; you could tell it was small talk. Then, from out of nowhere, my father looked at me and said:

'If you don't like school then leave. Get a job like your brother, an apprenticeship, and start earning money. What's the point of continuing at school if your results aren't there?'

I was taken aback; even though my grades weren't at the highest level I had never thought about leaving. I had never had a job or worked in my life. My brother had summer jobs working in pizza joints in his early years, so he kind of knew what to expect. But me, I had never worked in my life so I had no idea what to expect. Furthermore, what would I do?

It took a few days for the idea of me working to simmer and agree that it might be a good option to take my father's advice and leave high school. My brother had done it; he seemed happy and it was working for him so why not me, right?

A few weeks later I sat down with my father and we discussed my options. He asked if there were any particular fields I was interested in. I wanted to say 'the arts' so badly. It was on the tip of my tongue as the only true area of work I wanted to pursue. But the conformity and the fear of: *You can't earn a living from art* was stronger than my will to voice an opinion. So I simply said 'no'.

The local paper happened to be next to him at the time. We opened the careers section and there was an ad for an apprentice butcher. 'People are always going to eat meat' said my father as we studied the advertisement. 'Yeah, I guess' I replied. 'Well there's no guessing; you either get a job or improve your grades' my father said in an angry, direct tone.

Who was I kidding? We both knew my grades weren't going to improve unless they incorporated animation into every subject. So, before I knew it, we were constructing a cover letter and the smallest resume that has ever had been submitted, as there was no previous work history to be outlined.

Two weeks later when I got home from school there was a voice message flashing on our machine. As soon as I walked in I pressed it and there it was, the butcher position I had applied for. I landed an interview. I had mixed emotions; I wasn't excited or happy, I was just stunned. I mean, I never in my wildest dreams saw myself in the workforce at such a young age, and now I was faced with the prospect of carving up a pig's rear end for a living. I just couldn't fathom that.

I took the interview. It was pretty formal as the company was a large supermarket chain and the butchery department lay within that. I answered the questions as best I knew how for a fifteen-year-old who had never been interviewed in his life.

My father drove me to the interview and waited for me outside the entire time. 'So how did you go?' 'Yeah, good I think. I guess we will find out soon enough,' I replied.

Three days passed before I again returned home from school to see the answering machine flashing. I wasn't so keen to hear the message this time round. After staring at it for a while I pressed play: *Hi Matt, this is John from the butchers. After deep consideration, we would like to offer you the position of apprentice butcher, starting in one month's time. If you could give me a call back to go over the finer details, thanks Matt.*

I couldn't believe what I had just heard. Once again, I wasn't happy; the only emotion I felt was confusion. Did I really want to leave school and become a knife wielding, meat cutting butcher? Absolutely not! But in theory (there's that word again 'theory') it made sense.

When my father returned home that day and heard the message he was over the moon. I had never seen him so happy. It was as though he had won the lottery. I couldn't tell him that this wasn't what I wanted to do and I really didn't want to accept the position. I felt I had disappointed him enough with my grades. I couldn't disappoint that hardworking person who had provided for me even more.

The next day I went to school and took all the necessary steps and procedures to leave and enter the workforce. To my surprise, most teachers expected this outcome from me and not many were shocked to see this as my next move in life. There was only one person who was shocked and tried to talk me out of my decision and that was my art teacher. When I told her I was about to leave in two weeks it was as though all her worlds had come crashing down: 'Are you sure? What are you going to do? Will you continue your art? Why don't you stay and continue with art studies at university?'

University!! Was this woman crazy? I was barely passing high school and she is talking about university, plus it was instilled within me that art was for hippies and dreamers and not for people who wanted to make a living in life. 'Yeah I'm sure; don't worry I will continue my art. Thanks for everything Miss, see ya!'

Those were my final words to the only person who supported my true passion in life at that time. A short quick hug and I would walk out of the only classroom that put my soul at ease and allowed me to express my hurt, confusion, pain and joy, while creating beautiful pieces of art that students and teachers would talk about for hours. I was off to enter the workforce, to a job that I had no interest in. This would be my first encounter with the harsh side of life and a real reality check. For someone who was a fresh as a T-Bone steak you'd just purchased from your local butcher, I was about to be carved up with the sharpest knife in the chopping block.

Chapter 4

The Colour of Abuse

Now you will need three boning knives and one butcher's knife, along with a mesh glove to be worn at all times when 'on the knives'. For the first year, as you are only fifteen years of age, it is illegal to sell knives to you so you will have to use the senior butcher's knives until you come of age.

*O*rientation for my apprenticeship lasted one full week; just me in a room watching videos about occupational health and safety, the rules of the company, how to handle difficult customers and, of course, the interaction between workers and the respect that comes with working in a large supermarket chain. I was going to be working within only one section of the supermarket but the rules were universal for every section, so everyone sat through the same orientation process.

The company appeared structured and well-organised and the person in charge of my orientation seemed well-educated; not very happy, but well-informed. As my place of employment was within the butchery department, there were a certain number of extra responsibilities and rules that applied as we were handling knives. And not just your everyday salad-cutting knives; these things were like machetes, flesh-destroying tools.

It was illegal to sell knives to a minor, even if working within that particular field or trade. So I was clearly told that I could not buy knives as part of my tools of trade until I had turned sixteen. Sitting in the orientation room, that didn't make a whole lot of sense to me. Wasn't I hired to cut meat as a butcher? If I could not do that, what else would I be doing?

As someone who had never entered the workforce before, I guess you could say I was quite naive. I was excited and thought this job was going to be a breeze for the first year; I would be doing nothing and getting paid for it. I was looking forward to the prospect of this new canvas I was about to paint, so to speak.

The job would see me starting work every day at 5am; the butchers were first to start, as there was a lot or preparation to be done before the supermarket opened at 8am sharp. I didn't drive at the time as I wasn't old enough to hold a licence. Fortunately for me, my father worked around the corner from my job, so he dropped me off and picked me up every morning and afternoon as our start and finish times were near enough the same.

'Are you ready son? First day of work, just give it your all, show your enthusiasm and all will be well,' I can remember my father saying, at 4.30am on the first day in the car. I was nervous, as I didn't know what to expect. Only a month before I was high fiving my friends at school, drawing every day, living with no real worries or hassles. Now I was about to walk into a room full of guys that I had never interacted with, didn't know from a bar of soap, and I had no working experience to refer back to.

I couldn't show my father that I was scared. I didn't want to look weak in front of a guy who had been in the workforce since the age of fourteen. I don't remember him ever having a sick day; even if he were sick, he would still go to work, provide for the family and always seemed relatively happy. I loved him too much to let him down, so I simply kept quiet and smiled. So I grabbed my backpack, gave my father a hug and walked into the dark alleyway where the after-hours entrance was.

I can remember looking back at my father just as I was about to walk in and giving him a wave. To this day I can clearly see the glow in his eyes, as though he were proud to see his youngest son enter the workforce. It was a bittersweet experience for me. I felt for the first time in ages that I was making him happy but deep down within myself I wasn't happy. I didn't want to be a butcher, my anxiety was high, and something inside was telling me not to do this; to go back to school and study hard, this wasn't my path. But as we mostly do in life because we are not trained to listen to and harness our inner indirect teachings, I ignored that little voice inside and all the negative feelings that were attached. I gazed back at my father, smiled, gave him a wave and walked into an 'institute'. I still call it that to this day, because that's how my vision was distorted to view it. I began the first transition of my life and felt real pain and turmoil.

'Boys, this is Matt our new apprentice. Let's make him feel welcome'. The butchery department consisted of a boss who was an ex-boxer and looked like the hulk with no hair, a second in charge who could have been a basketball player with his height and two middle-aged tradesmen who were quite large in stature. I was the skinny 55 kilo fifteen-year-old kid, a fresh piece of meat in my own right.

All the guys were of Australian descent with fair skin and hair and blue eyes. Then there was me, total opposite, European descent, dark olive skin, brown eyes, still sporting that puberty moustache my father would not allow me to shave.

I didn't think much of the culture difference and my ethnic appearance, as I hadn't encountered any negative experiences or racism in the past with the way I looked. So there was no reason for that type of threat to be in my thoughts.

Well, that was my immature, inexperienced, untrained mind not allowing me to see; not looking beyond a painting to see the true meaning, where the painting was inspired from, and how it got to be so beautiful. Instead I looked at the image (in this case the other butchers) and saw them for what they were, people just like me. In the workforce, that's a very dangerous mindset to have, especially in my world at that time.

One of the tradesmen I kind of clicked with was 27 years old, a nice enough guy and, as we learnt more about each other, he seemed cool and we found common ground as we both practised martial arts. I had started when I was seven years old with my older brother and continued for the next ten years in various styles including karate, kickboxing, kenpo, Muay Thai and kung-fu.

You see I' always loved practising and developing my skills in martial arts. I'm not sure where the passion came from but I was a natural. My form was perfect but I didn't liked confrontation, though I knew how to protect myself physically.

Even when being bullied at school, every time he grabbed the back of my neck so violently I could see myself gripping him in a particular headlock, pinning him to the desk and cutting off his circulation with one move, yet I never followed through with that vision.

That's the thing with martial arts; there's a very strong discipline element attached. Every school that my brother and I trained at was very strict on this policy. So if they found out that any student was fighting outside the dojo we would pay for it at training. And that's one place you wouldn't want to mess around, as every fighter at the time was highly skilled and would hurt you in ways that would see you limping or black-eyed for weeks after.

During the first six months of my apprenticeship, the work was repetitive. Every morning I would prepare eight different types of mince, ready for the 8am rush. I would then unload the trucks that brought in the stock, stack prepacked meat on the shelves and spend the rest of my time packing sausages, wrapping meat onto trays and, of course, cleaning.

It was hard work, especially for someone who had never worked a day in their life, but I can actually say that at the beginning I was enjoying it. The pleasure would soon be cut out of me, just like the rump of a cow being carved up into slices of thick juicy steaks ready to be gnawed on by hungry carnivores, leaving the remainder of the rump to be mixed, crushed and turned into leftover mince. That leftover mince would be my soul, my spirit that they would carve out of me as they tried to turn me into someone I wasn't. Each day I was tested, the devil or devils were about to show their true colours and see how far my pain barrier would allow me to survive in their house of hell. The colour of abuse was about to be painted all over my canvas.

'Hey Matt. when are you buying your own knives so you can start cutting; you're not using mine!!' one of the tradesmen rudely lashed out one morning, as I was preparing the mince. 'I have to wait until I turn sixteen to buy knives as it's illegal for me to purchase anything right now' I replied, in a subdued and somewhat confused voice. Why was he being so rude to me and asking such a question? He had been a butcher for over thirty years; shouldn't he know such menial information? Why did he ask such a stupid question? 'Don't be a pussy; how are you supposed to work without knives? What a joke!!' he continued to rant and rave for the rest of that day. I kept quiet with mixed emotions.

Did I do something to make him angry? Was he having a bad morning? Did he have an argument with his wife the night before, so he decided to take it out on me the next morning? All of these questions would continually be painted on my mind. I kept quiet that entire day and left work in a cloud of confusion. My father could see something was wrong at the dinner table that night but I assured him everything was okay and said I was just tired. 'Get used to it son; that's the workforce' my father said jokingly.

That night I locked myself in my room and began to sketch. I hadn't picked up a pencil in months. I had neglected my saviour and true passion in life, my art. It seemed to be the one element that would always find its way back into my life, as though the angels were depositing my peace in front on me when I couldn't voice my pain to my parents. I drew so much that night I fell asleep at my desk and woke to the alarm blaring in my ear, telling me it was time to get ready for work.

I had forgotten about the incident with the angry butcher—that's what I secretly nicknamed him. I hoped he'd be in a better mood that morning and not ask such meaningless questions nor feel the need to verbally abuse me. That hope would soon be just that … hope.

The angry butcher was on a mission, a mission to pull every emotional chord I had and see how far he could push me; even worse, if he could push me overboard.

'Good morning, pussy' was his daily morning greeting to me. Loud, sharpening his knife and staring directly at me with a glare of hatred, as though I had killed his mother or slept with his wife. I thought maybe I should do one or the other—at least then he would have an actual reason to hate me.

I didn't know what to say. I was so scared—scared he would lash out again or make a fool or me in front of the other butchers—so I didn't say anything and went straight on to prepare the mince.

'Didn't you hear me? I said, "Good morning, pussy"!' There he was, an inch away from my face. I could feel his hot smelly breath on me. At least 140 kilos of pure body fat, red face, blood all over his apron and smelling as though he had bathed in pig lard, standing in front of me. To be honest, I thought he was about to stab me, so my martial arts switch flicked on. I immediately stood back and, in the quietest trembling voice, said 'Good morning.'

As soon as I greeted him he went back to his chopping blocks, smiled and continued to carve up his subject. What was going on? Obviously the incident the day before wasn't a one-off, so why wasn't the boss saying anything to him, why were they all laughing? All of these things raced through my head as I prepared my daily mince. I would soon find out they weren't my friends, they weren't even my work colleagues, they were the force of evil testing my faith and my belief in myself. This was life's first lesson about to be handed to me from the textbook I would compile over the years and title *The University of Life's Teachings*.

Now don't get me wrong … university seems to work for most. But where my argument lies is that most of the time spent is all theory based, meaning there are no 'real life' practical experiences. From speaking to others, troubleshooting is not taught in your field of study, so it is near impossible to learn how to deal with every scenario out there, as a new situation is created every minute.

On graduation, an individual leaves with the most expensive piece of paper with their name on it, to be hung in their parents' lounge room as a trophy or prize in its own right. But the individual leaves with a distorted vision of life and a conformed way of thinking, developed through the processes of yet another conformed institute.

I obviously did not attend a formal university, but the degree I have earned is one of the best that life can offer. It may not be hanging on any wall in a nice frame, but I can assure you that the lessons I have learnt and the experiences I have been thrown into have developed my mind, especially today in business. I will illustrate further how it has enabled me to open doors at a very young age—no University system could have taught me.

Back to the angry butcher … he had started his rampage against me only one year into my apprenticeship. The feelings I had walking in the entrance when my father dropped me off for the first time resurfaced. Those feelings of uncertainty about this not being the path I needed to travel down all hit home. A stream of panic flooded my body, as though a tin of paint had just been thrown on a brand new car. It felt as though I had been punched in the guts with an iron fist.

Over the next six months, my days would include verbal abuse and names I wouldn't repeat due to the high level of racism, with me as the direct intended target. It was happening all over again, a pattern that would continue for years. It was the bully all over again but this time they had knives, they were a lot bigger than I was and my brother wasn't there to save me. This was the boxing ring of life and there was no white towel to throw in; just me and my will to fight and not give in.

After continuous months of abuse, it wasn't just the angry butcher. Now it was the whole department, even the boss. The only person who gave me some sort of comfort was the second in charge, the one who should have been a basketball player. I could see he wanted to help at times and would send me off to do other jobs when the boss wasn't around. I knew it was his way of taking me out of the line of fire. But for some reason he would never actually stand up for me. He would just watch from the sideline until one day he had no choice.

It was just after lunch. The tradesman and boss had started early that morning so they were finishing early; the second in charge and I were to work our usual hours. The second in charge had just left for his lunch break. Our lunches were an hour long but this hour would seem like ten for me that day.

'Hey pussy, go and get me some rump! I have an order I need to fill before I go; hurry up'! Those words fired across the room from the mouth of the angry butcher.

I was sweeping the floor at the time. There was so much inside me that wanted to use my martial arts training and grab that broom and wrap it around his neck. But I knew better. I kept sweeping, as there was quite a bit of rubbish around and I wanted to get it done in case the boss got angry at me for not keeping the department clean.

Then it happened. My first life-threating experience would see me become engulfed in the flight or fight mode for the first time in a work situation. When I finished sweeping, I put the broom down and walked into the cool room to collect the requested rump. The cool room wasn't big and was full of shelves, one little light, a rail to hold the carcasses and was minus 10°, as it needed to house meat at the correct temperature to allow for the longest shelf life.

You had to wear an insulated safety jacket each time you entered, otherwise you would nearly freeze to death. For some reason this time round, I couldn't see any jackets hanging up for me to wear. I didn't want to mention that I wasn't going in there without a jacket, as the angry butcher would most likely stab me, so I just walked in to retrieve his request.

I hadn't been in there for more than a minute when I heard the door slam shut. There he was, the angry butcher! I had my back to him as I was opening a fresh box of rump. I turned around and he grabbed me, pinned me to the shelf and held his sharpest knife to my throat. The meat in my hand fell to the floor; it was like watching it fall in slow motion as in a scary movie, waiting for the superhero to save the day.

'Now listen here you little shit; when I tell you to do something you do it straight away. And if you want to go and run your mouth off about this little incident, next time I wont just hold the knife to your throat, I will slice it open so you bleed to death like the pig you are!'

I froze; I had no idea what to do. Should I scream? Well that wouldn't help, the cool room was insulated. Should I punch him and run? Well that wouldn't work, because my hand would get lost in his fat. And I couldn't utilise my martial arts skills because, if I did, only one person would have walked out of that cool room alive and that would not have been the angry butcher. I was not going to risk going to jail for him, so I didn't say a word. He put his knife away, gave me a slap in the face and walked off.

I had no idea what to do or say when I walked out. I was far from an actor so how could I pretend that I had not just been threatened with a knife to my throat and how was I going to continue to work there? Worst of all, what would my father think?

When I was younger, I always worried about what other people would think, especially my family. I think it's because of the tight bond we all have. But that characteristic would spill over into nearly every area of my life, especially my art, as I grew older.

I can remember that when I completed a painting or sketch, I would always show my family. Each time a reaction of surprise and pride were etched on my parents' and brother's faces: 'Matt this is great; so much detail, you should be proud.'

That's the thing I would never be proud of my work. I was my own worst critic and never satisfied with anything I did. That became stronger as my confidence was stripped through my place of employment. It led to the biggest and most ill threat to everything I had become and worked for as a person for my family to be proud of.

The University of Life had the greatest exam ready and waiting for me. But if I failed, I wouldn't simply be able to re-sit this exam, people would be attending my funeral instead, as I would fail the most important lesson needed to survive.

I took three minutes to gather myself that day in the cool room. I can distinctly remember it was three minutes, because I watched every second pass by on my watch.

It's funny because that life experience (or indirect exams) have stayed with me throughout my working life. When I speak to clients and book a potential meeting, or speak with them through email or even in person, I catch myself being detailed and requesting only three, seven or eleven minutes of their time—really specific lengths of time. People always reply, 'Wow that's precise!' and I smile internally, thinking back to the day my throat was nearly opened by a man that didn't care about me or the value of my life to myself and my family.

The three minutes were up. I went to pick up the whole rump that I had dropped and noticed it wasn't there. I didn't really pay too much attention to it, as everything was a blur. *Maybe I put it back on the shelf?* I thought to myself. So I simply grabbed another one and made my way back into the butcher department to face my next serving of abuse.

As I went to exit the cool room and tried to yank the door open, nothing happened. I though it was jammed, so I yanked on the handle again. Nothing. So I started to knock, yelling 'Hey the door won't open, I think it's jammed!'

I waited for a minute but no-one came. How could I have expected anyone to rescue me, considering the savages I worked with. I continued to knock and scream until bang! The light went out. The door wasn't locked or jammed ... I had been locked in the cool room and it was only fifteen minutes into the second in charge's lunch break and the angry butcher had gone for the day. Hell had literally just frozen over and I was in it.

With no jacket to keep me warm, the first survival element of my brain started to kick in. I needed to keep warm, that was my only concern. I didn't need to worry about food; I had plenty of meat around me. I gazed around the small dark cool room but couldn't see a thing.

Mobile phones were not allowed in the work place but, due to the constant abuse at that time, I secretly had it in my pocket on silent at all times. Awesome! I would just call someone to save me. Wishful thinking, as I found there was no mobile service in the cool room, so that lifeline quickly disintegrated.

So I did the only thing my untrained mind allowed me to think of. I opened several boxes or meat, wrapped the empty cardboard boxes around my body and placed another eight layers of cardboard on the cold concrete floor, as my legs were weak from the stress my body had been through when the knife had been at my throat. I kept locking and unlocking my mobile phone, to keep the light on the small screen to generate small amounts of heat on my face.

I didn't care about any radiation that the mobile phone light could cause so close to my face. All I was worried about was staying warm. There I was lying on a cool room floor, covered in opened cardboard boxes as a form of insulation with a mobile phone near my face, trying to keep warm and not die from the freezing temperature in that cold coffin.

I really thought I was going to die that day. Looking back, I really don't think I could have died from the temperature in the cool room. But I was a scared kid who had been constantly abused for the past year; I wanted to die, if this what life was about. If this was what life had in store for me, then I didn't want to be a part of it. I wanted to stop worrying, stop caring and stop being so nice for once and just be rid of the harsh world. Hopefully, I would reach a nicer place in the afterlife.

I fell asleep in the cool room. I must have provided enough warmth for my body to actually feel a little relaxed, only to wake up to the frantic second in charge shaking my shoulders and screaming my name, to see if I would respond. 'Matt, are you okay?' When I didn't react he said, 'Let me call someone,' to which I quickly responded, 'NO!' I went on to inform him what had happened. He sat with me on the floor and consoled me as by that time I had burst into tears and was shaking uncontrollably.

He then looked at me and I will never forget what he said. His 'under the table' guidance saved my life. 'Matt. they did the same thing to me when I first started. They want to show you who's boss. But I must be honest, I wasn't treated as badly as they are treating you.' He went on to tell me stories of what they used to do to him. He was right, it was nothing compared to how they were treating me.

'You need to fight fire with fire sometimes. Your friends are still at school, right? The butchers are ganging up on you like school gang fights, and you are the new kid in the playground. Now I am far from suggesting any physical violence' … and here was the kicker he went on to say … 'Go home and call all of your friends still in school. Come into work tomorrow like nothing has happened, straight away that will shock the butchers, then when your friends finish school early, get them to come in and say hi. Okay Matt? Just get them to come in and say hi.'

I was picking up what the should–have-been basketballer player was putting down and, for the first time in a long time, I felt a rush of positive adrenaline race through my body. I jumped up, grabbed my stuff and rushed home. I didn't even wait for my dad. I called him, mentioned I was going to a friend's house after work (which I was) and my plan was about to be set in motion.

I didn't get home till late that night. I was at my friend's house organising my 'visit' at work, which had to go down the next day. I got home and went straight to bed. That night I couldn't sleep; I was nervous, scared, excited and a million other emotions raced through every cell of my body. I eventually fell asleep, only to wake two hours later.

The next morning I was ready. I had arranged with one of my closest friends to bring about ten guys to my work; not do anything, just 'show a presence'. I jumped out of bed and put on my invisible armour, as if I was ready for war. The angry butcher and his henchmen wouldn't know what was about to hit them.

'Good morning fellas' I said, walking into the meat department that day with the most confidence I had ever felt. It was a facade; deep down I was still scared. But throughout my life, when the higher source has needed me to, I have put on my coat of ego and not let anything get in my way.

The morning was relatively quiet. I am sure the whole department knew something was going on. How could I have been so happy with what had happened just yesterday and, better still, how could I have the balls to show up for work that day?

At 1pm, everyone was in the department, including the angry butcher, and my army was close by. 'Matt, there's a few guys here to see you.' 'Oh really,' I replied, in a surprised but knowing voice.

I approached the window to see the ten friends I had organised to instil a little fear into my archenemy. But to my surprise there were about forty guys total standing there in uniform—even I was intimidated.

I walked out to greet my closest friend and looked at him as if to say, 'Who are all these people?' But I acted cool, as though I knew them all. About five minutes later, I noticed the angry butcher come to the window. I'm sure he intended to yell some further abuse at me but, as he approached, a guy within the group who I didn't know too well yelled out: 'Is that him? Is that the fat piece of shit? Come here hot shot and I'll show you who's boss!'

Then it was on and a few other guys started to get fired up. On the one hand, I was happy because these guys who I really didn't know were standing up for me; but on the other hand, I didn't know them and I didn't know what they were capable of. The scene quickly escalated, security came and, of course, the big boss of the entire store.

My friends were forced out of the supermarket and I was summoned to the boss' office; just like school, when I was kicked out the classroom for being a clown. Except this time no-one was laughing. I was forced to explain what had happened to me with regard to the knife incident.

This is where it got interesting—another of life's lessons was waiting for me to embrace.

'Matt, I'm going to give you a warning; any more of this behaviour and you're fired!' Those words slowly penetrated my soul, as if everything that had happened stemmed from me being a troublemaker. Was he serious? Did he not hear the entire story about my life being threatened and me being locked in the cool room yesterday? 'Now go home for the day and you can come back fresh tomorrow.' I got up angrily, slammed the chair, ripped off my butcher's coat and threw it at him, then walked off. Luckily my friends were waiting for me and we all went back to one of their houses to settle down.

I received a message on my phone: *Come home now.* That's all it read; it was from my mother. She was never short when messaging, there was always *I love you* or some sort of heartfelt wording to brighten up my day. But not today. I knew they had found out what had happened; it was time to face the chopping block.

I walked in the door and there they were: Mum, Dad and even my brother. 'Sit down!' my father said in a firm voice. 'Do you want to tell us your side of the story?' he asked, so I did. I broke down in a stream of tears and told them every little detail.

After about an hour my story was finished. I had a pile of tissues next to me and there was silence in our lounge room. My father was sitting on the opposite couch at the time; he got up and walked toward me. *Great,* I thought, *I am about to cop a beating from him now, and I couldn't get my friends onto him.*

My father grabbed me and held me tight. He spoke softly like an angel whispering in my ear, 'Don't worry son, you don't have to work there anymore. I have arranged to have you released from the apprenticeship. I don't want you there anymore.'

All of my fears and high levels of anxiety about going to work and being abused for no apparent reason were over, just like that. I could now live a normal happy life again.

I had no idea what I was going to do; but at that time I didn't need to. All I needed to know right then and there in my father's arms, with my mother bawling her eyes out and my brother hugging her, was that family was number one. They are the ones who will stand by you no matter what. This would become the most important part of the next attempt to take my life, later on in my journey on this physical place we call Earth.

A few weeks later, I had to go into the supermarket to sign the release papers. But I didn't need to go anywhere near the meat department, so I was okay with that. I walked in with my head down; I was sure everyone knew what had happened and were creating their own gossip channels among themselves. But I didn't care about them, as I knew my truth.

I had to walk through the lunch room which heightened my anxiety a little, as I did not want to run into any members of the meat department. As I approached, I put my head down and walked at speed.

'Matt, hey Matt stop!' It was the second in charge should-have-been basketball player. I knew his voice but didn't want to stop, just in case the others were close by. He grabbed me, 'Hey I'm on lunch now. Meet me in the food court, okay?' I didn't want to meet this guy anywhere. Sure, he was the only one who was nice to me, but I had lost trust in humans. I didn't know if he was twisted and, with the angry butcher and his henchmen, maybe it was part of their plan to have him befriend me and deliver the final blow.

Despite such distrust, there was something inside me that said meet him, so I did. I ended up spending most of his lunch break with him. He told me that he had actually called my father weeks before the incident happened, so he could keep an eye on me at home. Then, if he saw any sudden changes in my personality, he would know why. He also went on to tell me that the big boss of the entire supermarket was best friends with the boss of the meat department. That's why nothing would ever happen to them; they had the system under their control.

The painting on the wall was a lot clearer to me and made a lot more sense. But it didn't matter; it didn't eliminate the fact that I was threatened and didn't give me back my sense of peace. I didn't really care. He gave me a hug and his phone number to keep in contact. I then left him to make my way back to the only place that would be my saviour … home.

I didn't stay in contact with the should-have-been basketball player. As a matter of fact, I threw his number in the bin immediately after we parted ways that day. I didn't want anything to do with that part of my life anymore.

At the time, I just wanted that part of my life erased and to start again; to start fresh and forget that painful element of my life. What I did not know is that pain is the first subject at the University of Life's teachings in becoming street smart. I was about to embark on not only the highest degree in street smart education but also my Masters in two areas where I would always find comfort in times of pain and turmoil: music and art.

Starting from Sketch

Where are you going tonight Matt?'

'I've got a friend's party from school; it's safe Mum, don't worry.'

After the whole butcher experience, my mother was quite concerned about me; I didn't go out much and didn't work for about six months. I had enough money saved and hardly had any expenses at the time as I lived at home. I could see my father was getting a little frustrated with me being home all the time and not working, but I think he was treading lightly. I was still rather quiet and those past negative experiences would revisit my mind uninvited.

I didn't know what I was going to do workwise; to be honest, it was the furthest thing from my mind. It was as though I had to start from 'sketch' (the beginning) all over again workwise. Looking for a job and getting my resume together brought on immediate anxiety, just thinking abut the entire process. I would revert back to the abuse I went through and instantly put job hunting on the backburner, returning to my art.

It was a Saturday night and I was about to be picked up by a friend to go to a house party, the first outing I had attended in six months. It was an eighteenth birthday for a girl who used to be in my year at school.

I didn't really want to go and face the music, everyone asking how my job was. I didn't want to explain that I had been forced to leave due to abuse, but there was a strong inexplicable force within telling me I had to go, and this force injected excitement through my entire being.

My friend and I arrived at the party and there were cars everywhere, blocking the driveway, flooding the streets, and people scattered all over the house. I never got involved in drugs or alcohol, even though many were sure I had been exposed to them in my later years. Almost everyone at this party was using drugs or drinking but I didn't care. I was never pressured; these were friends who were just happy to see me after not being at school for so long.

'Matty, where have you been? There's no-one to make us laugh in class anymore!' I heard yelled across the room as I entered the party, with other friendly remarks from people I used to spend my days with. Sure, they were probably high as kites but I didn't care; they weren't angry towards me and that's all I cared about.

As I walked in the garage to scope the scene further, I was exposed to a form of expression that would have me mesmerised and see me build my confidence back up in the coming months and years for the world to see, allowing me to shine. This was a form of expression that made one person the centre of attention in a positive way. This person could control people with his hands, pulling on others' emotional chords. And the surroundings—pure happiness!

There they were … something I had never witnessed before but for some reason I was drawn to. Two turntables, a mixer, amplifier, two large speakers, a smoke machine, some disco lights and there he was, the DJ!

This guy was in a world of his own. There were only ten people dancing at the time but the DJ was loving it. You could see the angels were flowing through him and he was in his own heaven. That's where I wanted to be and to eventually own that space.

I sat and watched him for the remainder of the night. I don't think I took my eyes off him and I was sitting so close to the speakers my ears were ringing for two weeks after. But I didn't care because something this guy was doing flicked my inner inspirational switch. I needed to learn the art of DJ'ing there and then.

I had never played an instrument in my life. I loved music and had grown up with an older brother listening to R & B and hip-hop who extended his passion to me. We would sit for hours pretending to rap, wearing our hats backwards, with basketball jerseys and baggy pants. We weren't trying to be gangsters or anything of that nature; the music just resonated with us, so why fight it?

After the party had finished, my friend was ready to go and drop me back home. I begged him to stay a little longer. I needed to chat to this DJ and find out more, how I could get involved in the art of DJ'ing and turntablism, so my friend reluctantly agreed.

'Hey man, can you help me lift the speakers into my car?' asked the DJ. 'Absolutely!' I replied. Here was my chance to find out all the information I wanted to ask. When I was younger, and this carried through to my working years, I had a way of asking the right questions at the right time. I didn't know what I was doing at the time or what lessons life was teaching me but, looking back now, I see it as a process of elimination or troubleshooting.

'So how long have you been DJ'ing? How did you get into it? Where else do you spin?' I guess I should have paced my questions but I was too excited. I just needed to know how, when, why and **now**!

The DJ was pretty helpful considering it was just after midnight and I was pounding him with a million questions, when all he wanted to do was go home to bed. 'Let's go man, I'm done!' I yelled at my friend, who I found asleep on the couch. I knew my father would be calling any minute now, as my curfew was midnight sharp.

I scraped home before a phone call from my father, crept straight to my room and turned on my computer, searching for the DJ equipment that the party DJ had suggested I start with: two turntables, one two-channel mixer, a set of speakers, amplifier and a pair of headphones.

After two hours of searching, I came across a company that had just opened in a nearby suburb. I clicked their website to find **SALE** in big bold letters. My eyes were naturally drawn to it and it was as though the angels or higher source were painting a picture for me, this time in the form of music and on the computer screen.

There it was … the entire set-up I needed to start, including all wires, speakers, stands, even including a smoke machine and basic lighting, all for just over $3000. Now at the time I wasn't looking at DJ'ing as a form of work or business, it was pure passion. But if I'd a business mindset at that time, $3000 was not a lot of money to outlay to start one. But from the outside looking in (meaning my parents, especially my father), it probably didn't look too healthy. Any large outlay for someone who wasn't working, especially someone who had never played an instrument, wouldn't be a smart move.

I stared at the computer screen with my mind in two worlds. I wanted this more than anything and why shouldn't I? The money was in my bank. Sure, I wasn't working at the moment but if I practised every day I would become skilled quickly and, in turn, start generating income from parties. I would plead this exact case to my father the next day: if I practised every day and every night and put 100% of my entire being into it, I would be sure to get small gigs quickly. I wouldn't stop until I did; I just knew I had to do this.

I poured out my passion to my parents at the dinner table the next night. I don't think they had ever witnessed such passion and determination radiating from my soul before, and I am sure they could see the desperation in my eyes. 'I will think about it,' my father replied in his deep fatherly voice. But what was there to think about? I wasn't asking him for money, I just wanted to run it by them really. But with the respect that to this day flows through my veins, I quietly and happily said, 'Okay, thanks Dad' and continued with my dinner.

After dinner that night, I headed back to my room to do my usual art, drawing etc. Only an hour later, I heard my father's footsteps walking toward my bedroom. Instantly a rush of negative emotion took over. I thought to myself: *Here he comes, to tell me that the DJ equipment is too expensive and he doesn't want me to spend my money on it at the moment, while I'm not working.*

I braced myself, already fighting back tears from a situation that may or may not be the one I wanted. 'Matt, if you really want that stuff, on Saturday we can both go and have a look and buy it all, okay?' I will never forget that night when those words flowed from my father's mouth. I remember jumping up and giving him the biggest hug, bursting into a hysterical cry of happiness. 'Matt what's wrong; why are you crying? I said you could get them?' my father said in a worried tone. 'I'm just happy Dad, thank you.'

I think that was the longest I'd ever hugged my father. It was a build-up of so many emotions and knowing that he was there for me. After I'd stopped crying, my father wiped my dripping nose and said in such an angelic tone, 'Get some sleep son.'

I had the deepest sleep that night. I don't remember dreaming or waking up, all I remember was my father walking out of my room as he turned my light off, giving me the same smile he did the first day I walked away from his car to begin my hellish apprentice butcher position. Except this time there was only me and two turntables to answer to, and that was fine by me.

True to his word, when the weekend came we were off to check out my new career. Well, I didn't view it as a career. If I could pick up this form of entertainment and do one party a week I could earn enough money—even more than I was earning as a butcher—and start to build my confidence back up. That was my plan.

We arrived at the shop and I ran into the store with the biggest smile on my face. It's funny but I can still remember that day; I had such confidence. I knew what to buy, how it worked, how to use the equipment and what I wanted to achieve with it all. Yet I had never showed any interest in music before, besides listening to the boom box in my brother's room.

'Can I help you?' I heard to my rear. 'You sure can, I am interested in the package with the two turntables advertised on your website,' I replied confidently. By this time, my father had made his way into the store. I could see the confusion on his face, as he had no idea what any of the 'stuff' in the shop was for. But that was okay because I did; I had a knowing within and that was all I needed.

The salesman spent the next hour with my father and me going through the entire set up, the dos and don'ts, how to use it, and how to set up and pack down. I wasn't listening, I didn't care as I knew what to do. All I wanted to do was pay this guy, pack it all in our car, set it up in my bedroom and practise until I was the guy someone else was staring at all night, eventually asking me the questions about how I'd got to be the greatest DJ who ever lived!

'So how much?' I heard my father ask, interrupting the salesman from his in-depth sales presentation. 'Only $3250!' the salesman quickly replied. 'Is that the best you can do?' asked my father. 'Are you paying cash?' My father confirmed that we were.

Then the salesman just walked off. What in the world just happened in that tennis match of questions between my father and the salesman? Did my father just piss off the salesman so he was calling security to kick us out? A portrait of panic was instantly painted on my face. 'What did you say that for?' I angrily whispered to my father, thinking we had lost the sale because he asked for a cheaper price.

I'd had no experience in the art of negotiation, so I didn't realise there were large margins placed on items sold basically anywhere, and that it was a person's given right to ask for whatever it was you were buying for a cheaper price; and that nine times out of ten, he who asks reaps the rewards!

'I have just spoken to my manager. The best we can do, if you pay cash and take it all today, is $2900.' My father looked at me as if to say, 'Never question your father' and replied to the salesman in a confident tone, 'We will take it.'

I wasn't sure what just happened. All I knew was that within three hours I would be at home, set up in my bedroom and practising a new form of expression that had been inspired only a week before by a person I had never previously met.

I was a little ambitious and it ended up taking most of that afternoon to unload, setup and test everything. But as my father is a genius when it comes to fixing or assembling anything, he got it done and the next two months would see me only leave my room to eat and go to the toilet. The remainder of the time I practised at least twenty hours a day.

Two months of practice passed and I was invited to another party, this time a little more formal, at a wedding reception venue. I didn't want to go but then a light bulb moment hit me and I thought: *I need to go and check out who is DJ'ing.* So I quickly got dressed in the nicest clothes I had at that time and went.

The party was a friend of a friend's eighteenth, so I didn't actually know the person who was holding the party. But it was a 'bring your friends' event and I was one of those friends who would tag along most times with my friends, as they always knew where the hot parties were around town.

While my friend would say hi to everyone at the party, that didn't interest me. There was only one thing I was there for and that was to scope out the night's entertainment. And as I were about to find out, there wasn't any.

'Um, where's the DJ?' I rudely interrupted, as my friend chatted with the birthday girl. 'He bailed last minute, so we are just using my brother's stereo player.' Was this girl serious? I was embarrassed for them; there had to have been 300 teenagers and parents at this party and there was no form of entertainment, in particular a DJ. I was appalled!

'I can do it, I have DJ equipment. You don't even have to pay me.' As those words uncontrollably escaped my mouth I was about to enter a realm of the unknown. I had never performed formally at a party before; had never packed down and set up my equipment at another venue besides my house. To be honest, the first time all the glory had been my father's; I had just sat around breaking up boxes and waiting for him to finish. On top of that, I only had hip-hop and R & B music in my catalogue. But once again, I didn't care. If it was going to happen, it was going to be then and there.

'Oh really, that would be great! Would it take you long to go and get all your gear?' the birthday girl quickly replied. My friend looked at me with confusion and anger, not knowing how I was going to pull this off. 'Nope, I live twenty minutes away so I should be back within the hour.' We were off to pick up my gear and return to entertain a party I knew no-one at, with no idea how they would react to me setting up halfway through their celebration.

We returned to the party forty minutes later and had everything set up in under an hour. I didn't even stuff up the equipment or wiring; I was good to go.

My parents were out to dinner that night so I left them this quick note so they wouldn't think my DJ equipment had been stolen: *Mum, Dad don't stress; I have taken the equipment to DJ a party. Not sure what time I will be home, love you.* I can only imagine their reaction when they read the note. Probably the same thing that raced through my mind at one point during the night when the dancing was about to begin: *What in the world am I doing here?*

'Do you have a microphone?' 'Sure,' I replied, handing my new microphone to the father of the birthday girl for the speeches. This was great as it gave me a little more time to gather my thoughts and revert back to the two months of solid practice at home.

'And now we dance!' said the large Italian man, father of the birthday girl and probably the boss of the mafia. A huge crowd of alcohol-fuelled partygoers slowly filled the dance floor and I hadn't even started to play any music yet; my inner panic button had been pushed.

I can remember my friend standing next to me, looking equally as panicked as I. We didn't know how this was going to turn out and I think he had the hots for the birthday girl, so now I had even more riding on the night.

I grabbed the microphone off the Italian mafia-looking father, my friend switched off the main lights, I turned on my little three-colour disco lights and yelled, 'Are you ready to party?' A stream of cheers followed and I pressed play, with the first song that would change the course of my life forever.

Until that night, I had never realised how important preparation was. I live today by an important quote which reads: *Prepare your field, for the rain will come.* This quote proved to be somewhat of a heading for the remainder of my life but back then, without me knowing, the two months practising solid in my bedroom was me preparing my field, and that party would not just be the rain but the thunderstorm that would see my field prosper.

I played that night for at least three hours straight. I don't think the dance floor was ever empty, and I don't remember having enough songs to cover the length of that party. But I obviously did and, luckily for me, they enjoyed the only style of music I had practised.

The end of the night came, my ears were ringing, the balloons had deflated, the streamers were hanging off the walls and I was packing up my equipment with the biggest smile on my face, while my friend was out the back flirting with birthday girl.

'Thanks so much for saving us; it was an awesome night and you were great!' I heard from the rear, as I was rolling up my speaker cables. I turned to see it was the mother of the birthday girl. 'Oh, it was my pleasure.' I replied loudly, as my ears were ringing from the blare of the headphone music I'd had in my ears all night.

Then it happened. As I was rolling my speaker cables, the mother started to move closer towards me. At this point I thought she was about to give me a hug, which I wasn't too happy about as I was covered in sweat and my body odour could not have been too appealing. As she walked closer, she paused a metre away, raised her fist, opened it and there it was—$400 cash, all in $50 notes, which made it look like it was double that. She placed it straight into my shirt pocket saying 'Thank you' and walked off.

Did what I think happened just happen? Did I just do my first DJ gig and actually get paid for it? And not just paid, I mean paid big time! $400 was like a million bucks back then; it was twice as much as I was paid as a butcher and the best bit was I'd earned it all in one night.

I remember the feeling that raced through my body at that time. I have never touched a drug in my life, so I can only use this term as an expression, but it was pure ecstasy.

I quickly grabbed the cash, placed it in my wallet, packed my equipment into my friend's car and, before I knew it, I was lying in bed, my equipment all packed neatly into a corner of my room and my wallet fat with 400 bucks cash. I slept peacefully that night.

'Good morning all! How are we on this glorious day?' I sang, as I approached the dining room table to join my family at breakfast. 'What happened to you and your DJ equipment last night?' my father asked curiously.

'What happened you ask Father? Well, I will show you what happened.' I hopped, skipped and danced my way back to my room, floating on cloud nine and retrieved the $400 from my wallet, proudly displaying it to my family. I slammed the money down in front of my father, not in a malicious way, but to make him proud of me. Over breakfast I explained to my family what had happened the night before and how I came to have $400 cash in such a short amount of time.

My father didn't say much that morning nor did my mother. I think they were confused and maybe a percentage of their being didn't believe that I'd actually been paid to DJ, as I had never actually performed anywhere before. Their confusion and uncertainty resonated onto me, and all of a sudden I felt embarrassed and ashamed.

Now my parents never said they were embarrassed and ashamed but because they didn't show much enthusiasm, I saw their reaction as negative. So all of my happiness and enthusiasm were quickly diminished and the old feelings I'd had while working at the butchery resurfaced. I angrily collected my $400 cash that I had so proudly presented to my father, went into my room and began to sketch out my emotions as per usual.

How dare they? How dare they not be happy for me? Look what I have done; I have made double what I used to earn in one night, doing what I was inspired to follow and they aren't happy for me. How dare they!' Angry thoughts of confusion clouded my mind, as the house phone rang loudly.

'Matt, it's for you.' For me? I wondered who was calling me at home. I hadn't met anyone recently, I wasn't expecting anyone. So who could it be? *'Matt, it's for you!'* my brother screamed again.

I reluctantly went out to see who was at the other end of the phone. 'Hi, I got your number from a friend whose party you DJ'd at last night. I am having my party in two weeks and was hoping you were available for that.' I found myself on the phone to my first referral client; well, I didn't see it as that or call it that at the time, but that's exactly what it was. 'Could you hold while I gather my diary to see if I am free on that date?'

Who was I kidding, I didn't have a diary, I was definitely free that date but had to project that I was a popular DJ. 'I have just had a cancellation for that date, so I am free to DJ your party. Can you provide me with the details?'

The person on the other end of the phone went on to tell me how many people were attending, the location, time frames and style of music they were after. Then she concluded by asking how much that would be. Now I didn't have a price structure in place, I didn't know what to charge. Then I thought that as I was paid $400 the previous night when I wasn't even meant to be at the party, I'd quote $400 and see what happened. 'That's $400 to be paid on the night? Great, let's book it in,' she replied.

A few minutes later I hung up the phone, back in my state of bliss and forgetting any negative emotion from around the breakfast table. 'I just got booked for my first proper gig!' I jumped on the stool I was sitting on and gave a scream of excitement. *'oh yeah'* I followed.

'Congratulations son, well done!' There they were, the four words I needed to hear from the man I looked up to, my father. I then sat next to him at the breakfast table, forgetting what had happened earlier and the negative thoughts I had created in my own mind. I went on to explain what had happened the night before, leading to that phone conversation and the booking for my first proper gig.

After the first booked gig, I went on to DJ nearly every week. I received repeat business from each party, even multiple gigs from the same client's family, weddings, 21st birthdays, even christenings. If there was a party that was going down in my area I would be the 'go to' person and some weeks I earned well into the thousands.

One Sunday I woke up just after lunchtime still tired. I had DJ'd three gigs that week and finished at two in the morning the night before. I headed straight to the kitchen, made myself a bowl of cereal and sat on the couch watching TV with my father.

'How was last night?' my father asked. 'Crazy and I got paid extra to stay and play longer, so I earned a thousand bucks' I replied, and continued to eat my cereal. 'So tell me Matt, is this what you're going to do for the rest of your life, have long night's, sleep all day and no real career?' my father quickly replied, dismissing my comment on how much I'd made the night before.

I didn't know what he was so angry about. I was finally working, earning a lot of money and quite happy. But what I didn't see or chose not to see was how it may have looked through a parent's eye. I mean, here I was DJ'ing parties at all levels with no real experience, earning rubber band banks of cash weekly.

To me it wasn't odd because I knew what I was doing. I wasn't involved in any drugs, my high was the crowds getting off to my music, and I was earning a living. But my parents had never witnessed me at an event or experienced the heavenly feeling I felt. So unfortunately they judged and assumed I was doing the wrong thing. how could someone so young fall into that much money so quickly?

'You start looking for a proper job tomorrow' my father said, as he got up from the lounge and walked off to do his usual weekend gardening.

I didn't pay too much attention to him at that point as I was too tired. I ate my breakfast/lunch and went back to bed. That Monday when my father returned from work, I was in my room practising some new tricks on the turntables. He opened the door and showed me the local paper; more importantly, a circled advertisement he had highlighted during his lunch break. It read: *Apprentice Sign-writer Wanted.*

There was that word again, 'apprentice'. I had subconsciously linked negative emotions to that word. As my father walked out, I grabbed the newspaper clipping, chucked it on the floor and went on with practising my new skills for that week's eighteenth birthday party.

'Did you look at the job ad?' 'Yeah, it's not for me' I swiftly responded. 'Why not? It's sign writing, it's close to home, it's art based and you still have your weekends to DJ, if you still want to do that!'

My father had a point, well he had many good points but, most importantly, my weekends would be free to DJ. I couldn't stop doing the one thing that had built my confidence back after those dirty butchers had chopped it out of me.

So I applied and received a call back for the position within days. The owner of the company asked me to come in that coming Saturday for a trial, starting at seven in the morning.

The following Saturday morning I drove to the trial for the position of Apprentice Sign-writer. I spent six hours with the boss and his son, who was around thirty years of age at that time and had only ever worked for his father's company as a sign-writer.

The boss seemed cool, a hard worker. The work was fun, painting a few backgrounds in enamel oil-based paint. He taught me a few tips on how to make the paint appear as though it had a glass finish and he even bought me lunch that day.

'So what do you think? Do you like it here?' 'Yeah it's cool,' I replied. 'Do you see yourself working here?' the boss asked. 'Yeah, I mean it seems like something I would want to further my interest in and it's art based, a field I love' I replied. 'Great, you start Monday morning eight o'clock. I will have all the papers ready for you to sign.' Within minutes I had been offered and accepted a position as an Apprentice Sign-writer.

'How did you go?' my father asked anxiously as I arrived home. 'I got the job and start Monday.' My father jumped up and gave me a hug, 'Nice work son.' But once again I wasn't sure if I was happy. It had happened all too quickly to be honest; it was a similar pattern to the process of gaining the butcher position and we all know how that turned out. So forgive me if there was a layer of uncertainty this time around.

I didn't show any emotion; I joined in the family's celebration but not for too long as I had a party to rock that night. I can remember driving to the event that afternoon, with a carload full of equipment and mixed emotions. Don't get me wrong, I was happy that I had gained the position. It meant I would earn a second income. But there was still a level of anxiety flowing through my body.

Was it the bad taste left in my mouth from the butchery? Was I subconsciously worried it might happen all over again? On top of that, I was concerned that the full-time work would infiltrate my DJ life and not allow me to DJ as frequently, and that made me quite uncomfortable. I didn't want to stop or even ease off on the one thing that gave me the strength to wake up each morning and face the world.

With all of those doubts and questions that were racing through my mind, at eight o'clock the next Monday morning I embarked on a four-year trade in sign-writing. I experienced a life that most people would never dream of and just survived to write about it.

Chapter 6

Running Out of Paint

Man, you go to the toilet a lot Snifter. Have you gone to the doctor to sort yourself out, or are you just trying to get out of work?

I would hear the above tirade daily from the boss's son. He had given me the nickname 'Snifter', for what reason I never cared to ask. I am sure there was some sort of insult behind it, but I just didn't care to know.

My family tree shows a history of bowel problems, mainly what has been labelled today as irritable bowel syndrome. As far as I was aware it was never life-threatening, no-one had died from it. The core issue that seemed to be present throughout the generations, mainly in males, was frequent toilet usage and haemorrhoids.

I'd never really questioned it much growing up; I used to see my father using the bathroom quite frequently at home, so it became a normal thing for me.

I can remember walking home with one of my closest high school friends. He lived within walking distance of my home so we always walked to and from high school together.

We lived about a fifteen-minute walk from school and there was a certain spot about 50 metres from my home. It didn't matter what day or time it was and I could have eaten nothing all day. But as soon as I reached that particular spot, it was as though the gates of my bowel opened and nothing would stop it from blasting out.

Every day would see me with my keys ready to unlock the door—a form of forward thinking and strategic planning I would continue into my later years—knowing that as soon as I hit that spot I would need to sprint home, leaving the front door open for my friend to enter ten minutes later.

This problem continued into my working years, not as much in the butchery position as in the sign-writing apprenticeship. The urgency and frequency of my going to the bathroom increased and I wasn't really sure why. Again, I thought it was something that just happened.

Like most things in life, we miss the warning signs. Thinking back, I look at the situation with a grin as, quite ironically, for almost four years I learnt the art of signage—designing them and working out which colours and words appeal to the brain most effectively. Yet I missed all the warning signs that life was placing in front of me.

Having a bowel issue in school didn't really have too much effect on me, as each time I felt the urge I could easily run out of whatever class I was in, no questions asked and no real consequences, apart from missing the teacher babble on about things I wasn't interested in anyway. I didn't really have too many issues with my bowel while in high school. I really started to feel the change and effects when I started to work as an apprentice sign-writer.

In the real world, the working world, it's survival of the fittest, mentally and physically. Only the strong (or what I found out to be the ones who are selfish) survive. You leave your issues, whether personal or physical, at home and get your work done, as all that matters when working for someone else is time and money. You are replaceable and just another number. Well, that's how I was made to feel.

Within a year of working full-time during the day as an apprentice sign–writer, my DJ career catapulted and I became the 'it' DJ. I had made a name for myself. Everyone knew who I was, how successful I was at making a party rock until all hours, and everyone wanted me to be their DJ, no matter what I quoted. I hated my day job, so I put all of my energy into the parties I hosted and it started to show. I would show up for work on Monday morning half asleep, literally turning up right on starting time. It was school all over again. I worked five full days a week in the apprenticeship, then I would work four nights a week DJ'ing at a variety of events.

As I became more popular on the private event circuit, I gained some much-needed confidence and my first-up selling experience came into play. When I was being booked for a gig, I would offer another service of a sign or banner for the event for a small extra fee. Nine times out of ten, the client would agree.

So now I was working full-time during the day, DJ'ing multiple times a week, and also completing signs in my own time at home in the garage until all hours of the night. I would purchase the materials from a wholesale supplier, sometimes taking paints and brushes from work without the boss knowing.

I can distinctly remember a particular night when I was working on a 21st birthday banner, for a party I was to DJ that coming Saturday. I stopped, looked at the time and realised it was almost midnight. I felt panic race through my veins at the thought of going to work the next day to a job I wasn't really enjoying. Why was I working during the day in a job that I felt worthless in, when I was making twice the amount of income through my own signs and DJ'ing?

Although my thoughts made sense, I never voiced my opinion to anyone. I continued to wake up each day and make my way to a job that I was only doing to make my family happy, to show them that I was working full-time during the day in a secure position, just as generations before me had done. It was a proven system, right?

It's not that I didn't like the type of work I was doing; I was learning the fundamentals of sign-writing, which allowed me to complete jobs of my own with less responsibility than for the large corporate signage I was completing in my day work. I wasn't lazy; I was working two jobs and having only four hours sleep a day.

The element of this position that I didn't like, that would eventually spiral out of control, was a repeated process and situation that seemed to be a common thread of mine. It was beginning to affect my health in more ways than one.

In order for a small company to maximise profits, the owners practise work methods that save money any way possible, especially when it's a father and son business. This sometimes involves cutting corners. If you think about it, no-one will rat on them as they are family, so as long as a job is completed and the client is happy, no questions are asked.

A part of sign-writing which wasn't explained to me in my trial with the boss and, to be honest, had never crossed my mind, was erecting signage on the sides of buildings or wherever they needed to be. This involved the one thing I really didn't enjoy and had never been exposed to before, and that was heights.

Now I am not talking about screwing a sign onto a shopfront, while standing two or three steps up a household ladder. I am talking about multi-storey buildings and awnings on the sides of clubs, often situated on the busiest roads in Sydney. This was daredevil stuff.

We were hand sign-writing racecar dragway stadiums, and not at ground level. Sounds exciting, right? Well yes, if you are working off a safety-regulated elevated platform that has your safety covered. I would not have had an issue, despite my fear of heights, if my safety had not been jeopardised. But as mentioned, I was working for a father and son business and every cost was accounted for. So working off an elevated platform or scaffolding wasn't an option for them, as it would have eaten into their budget. In order to continuously win work from their competitors, they would quote low and not include any costs for safety equipment.

This father and son company didn't work off elevated platforms or scaffolding; their tools of choice, no matter how high the sign needed to be, were two ladders, planks and two L-brackets to hold the planks onto the ladder, and that was it! Oh, and rope to hoist the sign up as we stood in the middle of the plank, which bowed in the middle from the weight of two people, the signage and the drills and screws needed to get a sign mounted to the building as quickly as possible.

Added to the mix was unpredictable weather. No matter how sunny a day it was, as soon as I walked up those ladders it was as though mother nature was toying with me. The wind would instantly pick up and the ladders would sway from side to side as you were trying to winch a sign up and get a job done.

I remember a particular day as though it were yesterday. This day would be the beginning of my physical body entering a world of mental and physical combat; a form of combat that can literally paralyse you, bring you to your knees and not allow you the chance to fight back and defend yourself.

We arrived at a job in a new industrial estate. All of the factories were newly built and freshly painted, a business owner's dream. We arrived on site at 6am and the job was scheduled to be completed in less than four hours. 'Where's the sign going?' I asked the boss' son. 'Up there' he said, pointing to the top of the building. It would have been at least four storeys high and we had almost a ten metre sign to cover the entire front.

I was baffled that there was nothing on the roof of the work truck except two ladders and two six metre planks, secured by old hand rope. So I immediately sat back in the passenger's seat, thinking there would be an elevated platform on its way.

Prior to this, I never really ventured out on site to help; and if I did, it would be just to hand things to the boss' son. 'Is the boss on his way to help and bring the elevated platform?' I asked. 'No you idiot, why do you think you're here? Now untie the ladders!'

This was when my panic button within instantly signalled the alarm trigger; it was now clear that the boss' son and I were mounting these signs on the top of this building, with no elevated safety platform whatsoever.

As I untied the knots on the ladders, I was thinking through what I was about to do. Surely he didn't expect me to walk up that ladder alongside a building that looked so high I could have knocked on heaven's door and stopped in and had a coffee break with God, did he? All with a sign that weighed at least four times my bodyweight and simultaneously hold it securely to that building, balancing on a human foot-wide plank and holding on for dear life, all while he's screwing it to the building? Yep, that's exactly what he wanted me to do!

Reality set in as he said, 'Come here Snifter, I'll show you how to set up a ladder, L-bracket and plank; take your ladder over to your side and do what I do.' I couldn't believe what I was hearing; I didn't even know how to carry a ladder, let alone set it up with a plank. I knew there was going to be trouble and instantly started to feel pain in my stomach.

We often over anticipate a situation, way before we have lived through the actual experience. Sure, what I was about to do was dangerous, anyone could see that. I was about to walk up a four-storey building with no safety harness, just a foot-wide plank. And freshly-laid concrete was waiting for my body to paint its surface with a collage of body parts!

Life has lessons waiting for us each and every day. But lessons can only be learnt if they are difficult, if they really test our character, as pain needs to be felt in order to know what the freedom of joy feels like. Looking up to the top of that ladder, I was scared and worried about falling. I had never stood that high in my entire life, and it didn't help that my first height experience was about to be an unsafe one.

I was being taught a lesson by life; I was being delivered a direct sign. But I wasn't educated enough to see it as a sign. The emotional roller-coaster I had just embarked on was controlled by fear and anxiety, becoming stronger by the minute.

My physical body became affected and paralysed by the thoughts that controlled my mind. The lesson was there waiting for me to grab and use to my advantage; everything was pointing to it. But my body was paralysed, my mind was polluted with negative thoughts and my stomach was about as twisted as an electrical cord that I had rolled up the incorrect way after a gig and chucked in the back of my car, only to find months later shrivelled up from exposure to heat.

Too many of us allow others to dictate our lives; there is always that little voice within, constantly whispering and sometimes sending wrong messages. When it comes to our place of employment, that voice becomes ever more present and, if it jeopardises our position in the company, even if it is life-threatening, we ignore that voice and learn the hard way. Unfortunately, I didn't have much self-confidence as an apprentice. So I shut up and ignored all warning signs of what I was about to do.

My first step in the process was to winch up the ladder. Now this ladder wasn't any normal ladder, it had four sections to it which made it four times heavier. The trick was to lean the ladder on an angle along the building and just pull the rope to winch it up, so even someone as small as I was at the time could fully extend the ladder.

Next was the most excruciating part of the process, climbing up the ladder holding the L-bracket, which was made of solid steel and chain. Then the plank had to be positioned at working height. On this particular job, the L-bracket needed to be situated at the highest run of the ladder, almost four storeys high.

I did everything to avoid walking up that ladder. The boss' son was like a monkey; he was up to the third section of the ladder and about to make his way up to the final part to hook his bracket into place. He made it look like child's play. But it wasn't child's play and I was terrified. There I was, looking up while holding this heavy bracket in my hand and my entire body was breaking down. The pain penetrating my stomach was like a spear had punctured it.

'Hurry up, Snifter!' the boss' son yelled out but it didn't sound like a yell—he was so high up I could barely hear him. There was no escape; he had hooked his bracket and wasn't coming down to hook up mine. He was waiting there to ensure my bracket was in line with his; I had to do this.

I closed my eyes and said a quick prayer, just as most call on God's help in times of need. I placed the L-bracket over my shoulder and started to walk up the first run. I didn't look down, I just looked straight ahead, so my view the entire time was the newly-painted cream building. I was trying not to think too much as the higher I went, the more the ladder wobbled back and forth, which resulted in me panicking harder and my heart beating out of my chest.

I had never had so many components of my body working at the one time and not in a positive way. 'Hurry up!' he was now getting aggravated about the time I was taking to reach the top of the ladder. This didn't help my confidence … and then it all went sour.

As I reached the third section of the ladder, I looked down and, for the life of me, it felt as though I was standing on an outside ledge of a four-storey building about to commit suicide. Wait, hang on a minute, I was! I was standing on the side of a four-storey building, just not deliberately committing suicide.

I looked down and instantly my body came to a standstill and I froze. I wrapped both of my arms around the ladder and didn't take another step. 'Snifter, what the hell are you doing? Why have you stopped?' I didn't answer. I couldn't; my body had frozen, even my vocal chords had gone into hiding. All I can remember is opening my mouth to yell 'help' but nothing came out. It felt like my vocal chords had been cut.

'What the hell are you doing?' I heard again, angrily shot out of the boss' son's mouth. Then by some miracle, the words came screaming out of my mouth, 'I can't move! I'm scared, my body has frozen and I can't stop shaking!' 'Stop being a pussy, set the L-bracket and hurry up!'

There it was, that word that had been stuck on me like a clothing label that identified what it was, where it was made, and the name of the brand. Just over one year ago, an angry middle-aged butcher had stuck that label on me and left emotional scars that I didn't know were deeply buried, until I heard it again.

All of a sudden I felt rage, I felt anger and I saw red; I felt an instant sense of extreme fury. It was as though a thermometer was rising inside me from the heat of my anger and it wasn't going to stop when it reached the top.

'Hurry up, pussy!' Those words arrowed towards me, cutting me emotionally as they entered my soul. I slowly stopped shaking and started to make my way up the ladder one step at a time. I had a look of pure evil painted on my face, as though I was a soldier painted in camouflage, ready to enter the battlefield. All I wanted to do was wrap that L-bracket around the neck of the boss' son and hang him from that plank four storeys high, sign-writing the word 'pussy' on him in big, bold, black lettering.

I continued to progress further up the ladder. I didn't feel anything; I was numb. I finally reached the final section of the ladder, hooked the bracket into place, not caring whether it was in line with his bracket, and slowly made my way back down the ladder.

I think it took me about ten minutes to walk down my ladder after setting up the bracket, compared to the two minutes the monkey son took to fly down his. I finally reached solid ground and, as soon as my feet hit the concrete, it was as though a war had stopped as relief slowly flowed through my body. Then I went to take a step towards the car and my legs just gave way. I fell straight down, landing on my face. I didn't trip over anything, there was nothing in my line of sight, I simply collapsed from the amount of internal stress my body had placed on itself, using every ounce of energy to walk up the ladder.

The boss' son saw me fall but he didn't come to help me. All I heard was 'Get up pussy, now we have to put the planks up together. So hurry up, we are already running late and it's costing us money.' That's when I realised that these guys didn't care about me. I was near paralysed on the ground in front of this guy and he could see the fear that was painted on my face, but all he cared about was time and money.

Apart from the lack of concern this person had for my wellbeing, he continued to call me a name that was insulting in its own right, let alone one that brought back negative experiences from my past.

Rage started to kick back in. At this point, I was sitting on the floor with my knees close to my chest. I saw myself getting up and using my martial arts skills for the first time, not worrying about any punishment from the outside world. I just wanted this guy to feel the pain I was feeling; I wanted him to feel my wrath and I wanted to hurt him physically. The only way he was leaving this job site was in an ambulance.

'Let's go pussy!' That insult was the last draw and, from nowhere, I yelled 'No!!' I did it, I finally stood up for myself. It took my body reaching a physical and mental point I didn't know existed. I repeated 'No!!' followed by 'I will not climb back up that ladder; it's not safe! Is it even legal?' That was the key word, if only I'd known it earlier: 'legal'. As soon as that word projected out of my mouth, the boss' son stopped everything, looked at me, pulled out his phone and walked away.

I knew he was on the phone to the boss but I didn't care. I had been abused to a point where it had affected my physical body and the only thing I had some concern about was my father—what was he going to think? This is another problem facing the human race: we always seem to know or worry about what everyone else is thinking or is going to think, and we usually get it wrong.

I heard the car door close; the boss' son was sitting in the driver's side with the radio on full blast. Half an hour later, the boss turned up to the job site. I was ready for him to unleash on me, I was prepared. He parked his car, got out without even looking at me, and walked straight over to my ladder to continue with the job, setting up the plank and mounting the sign to the facade of the building.

Once the job was completed, the only words spoken came from the boss' son, demanding me to pack up the truck and get in. So I did, and we made our way back to the factory with not a word spoken the entire trip home, just the radio blasting.

When we finally returned to the factory the boss' car wasn't there. The job had taken most of the day and the factory was locked. I got out of the car ready to unload it, when I heard: 'Go home, see you tomorrow.' So I grabbed my stuff, hopped in my car, slammed the door and drove home.

That day changed me a lot. It taught me (well, tried to teach me) how to handle people, anger, act under pressure and deal with people ganging up on me. Those were the lessons waiting for me and, looking back now, I am grateful for them as I apply many of those teachings in the way I work today.

I arrived home that day very angry. I walked into the house slamming doors, not acknowledging anyone. 'What's wrong with you?' my father asked, as he entered my room to see what the commotion was about. 'Nothing, I am just tired and had a bad day.' 'Oh well son, we all have them.' I can remember thinking: *If we all have bad days like this, I now know why so many hate going to work. It's not a happy place to be, especially when the people around you make earning a living very difficult when it doesn't need to be.*

What my father wasn't aware of was that I didn't just have a bad day. I'd had the day from hell and this had been going on for some time; the intensity had just ramped up that day and, to top it all off, I was about to enter the dragon's den tomorrow and feel the wrath of the boss' bite.

I didn't eat dinner that night and fell asleep quite early. I was physically and mentally exhausted and there was a part of me hoping I wouldn't wake up to face what seemed like a family of angry butchers, just in the form of signs. This time they weren't holding knives, they used ladders and planks and verbal abuse to cut me open.

The next day I reluctantly threw myself back into the line of fire. I made my way to work and walked straight into the boss' office. There he was, sitting at his desk facing me as soon as I walked in. Our eyes met and his depicted an element of excitement; it was as though he was motivated to lay into me and I knew he wasn't going to hold back.

'So I heard you didn't want to walk up the ladder yesterday to do your job,' the boss threw at me, before I could plead my case. 'Well, heights are a part of this job; so if you can't do that, why are you working here and what are we paying you for?' I was thinking: *Great, don't pay me, fire me and I will happily move on.* 'Are you a girl or something?' There it was, not two minutes into the conversation and the abuse had started.

He went on yelling, pointing fingers and calling me names, both racial and derogatory.

This guy didn't get it; I didn't have a problem with working at heights and doing my job, my issue was with safety and cutting costs to get the job done. But you can't tell a raging bull when to stop.

That's what I wanted to say; that's what I saw myself saying. But as per usual I didn't; I kept quiet and continued to listen and copped verbal abuse, as though I was his own personal punching bag. About twenty minutes later he had finished his banter; I went out into the factory and continued to work.

For the next almost three years I continued to work there and was verbally abused daily, with names and insults that stripped my soul bare once again. I was manipulated by guilt to work at heights that made me vomit every time, from the fear I had built up internally. My boss had me doing the most demeaning jobs he could think of.

I can remember one particular day when there was no work on so, instead of allowing me to practise the art of sign-writing, he had me paint strip the bin in our factory. This was a round metal bin in our warehouse, used to throw out dirty rags. I had to use paint stripper with no mask or gloves. I had to remove all the paint from this bin, clean it with turpentine, then repaint it with oil-based paints. I completed that task within five hours. I can remember calling the boss to come and inspect the work, as he wanted to ensure I had completed it correctly. He came downstairs, looked at the bin, looked at me and said, 'Do it again!' There was absolutely nothing wrong with it and there was no reason for me to be even doing this type of work. He was just getting a kick out of punishing me and letting me know at all times who was boss.

That level of work and mind manipulation was what my daily activities consisted of, when the factory was low on actual work. At times he even had me at his own home, helping him renovate.

I felt so small I didn't want to face the world and my DJ'ing started to become affected. I still DJ'd regularly, but my energy levels were lowered. I didn't inject the same amount of passion and excitement into my parties. I was literally doing it for the money; the only way I could express my pain was through my art.

Those years were probably the hardest I ever had to deal with in terms of abuse. I thought I had put cruelty behind me when I left the butchers, but instead I had entered into a much crueller world. This world was even more dangerous, as I had nowhere to hide. The person who was pulling my strings was very intelligent; he knew what to say, when to say it and how to say it all, in a way that was indirect; but direct enough to hurt me emotionally.

I continued to suppress my anger. My release was through art and martial arts training, but they weren't enough. I had built up so much internal disruption that it was only a matter of time before it would break me.

I didn't want my family to know what was going on; there was a small part of me that felt maybe it was me, maybe I deserved the abuse, maybe I brought it on myself. After all, it was the same pattern that I'd gone through with the angry butcher. So a small part of me didn't want to make known what was happening, as I thought the outside world would see me as the cause. So I kept it to myself.

Every day I would be pushed to my limits at work; my pain, anxiety, fear and stress levels would reach boiling point, just in time to make my way home. I would calm myself on the journey home in the best way I could. I tried to put my mind in a state where I was able to speak to my family over dinner, not allowing them to see any pain, then I would cry myself to sleep every night.

At this time it felt as though I was 'running out of paint' so to speak; my soul was near non–existent. I felt no pain physically, I was numb to it.

I no longer enjoyed DJ'ing, even though I was about to perform at one of the biggest parties of the year—a 21st birthday with a crowd of nine hundred, a party I usually would have been pumped for the week prior.

It was the Saturday of the party and I had packed my car early that morning. I was usually pretty organised and liked to recheck everything just before I left for a gig.

I had a constant feeling of nervousness and anxiety in my stomach, not just for the party, it was an everyday feeling I had developed through such negative work experiences. I'd just learnt to live with it; my body had built a tolerance to pain.

I can remember it was exactly one o'clock in the afternoon. I needed to be at the party by five o'clock to set up. My clients' lived on acreage, with a massive garage where the party was going to be held. I had a good friend come with me every time to help set up. He would usually stay with me the entire gig, sometimes getting on the microphone to hype up the party, which I didn't mind.

I was about to have an afternoon nap before going to pick up my friend. I felt a sharp pain in my stomach, which made me stop in my tracks. I was lying in bed, my bedroom situated only two metres from the toilet. I ignored the pain as I did with every other pain and thought it would go away.

As I was about to close my eyes to try and get some sleep the pain returned, but this time it felt as though someone had stabbed me in the stomach with ten razor-sharp samurai swords, while simultaneously pushing a release button to my bowel.

I ran to the toilet, feeling an immense pressure in my stomach and my eyes. The pressure kept up for ten minutes straight and I felt anxiety, pain and sweated profusely.

When the pressure finally eased I checked to see what was in the toilet bowl. There was thick mucus-like blood on the sides and bottom of the bowl. Blood was continuously dripping from my anus and it didn't look like it was stopping anytime soon.

What the hell was going on? I didn't know what to do. Should I call out for help? Was I going to die right then and there? What was happening to me? I sat there watching the blood drip out of me, as though I had left the tap dripping in my sink or shower, that's how much blood was pouring out of my body. I could not believe my eyes!

I sat on the toilet for what seemed like hours but ended up being twenty minutes, which was a normal bowel movement for me. Anyway, no-one came to see if I was okay, which I was happy about. To be honest, if they had I wasn't sure how I was going to hide or explain what was going on.

The blood seemed to drip slower and slower. As it came to a near halt, I wiped myself as best I could, packed my underpants with toilet paper, flushed the toilet, cleaned the bowl and raced out of my house to pick up my friend and make our way to the party.

We arrived at the party three hours early, set up all of the DJ gear and hung around until guests started to arrive. Luckily we knew most of the people, so my friend could enjoy himself as we had arrived earlier than expected. Once we had set up, I sat behind my turntables pretending I was checking my music and ensuring all of the requests I had been asked to have for the night were in my playlist.

I wasn't checking for any songs; I couldn't stop thinking about what had happened to me healthwise just hours earlier in my bathroom. I knew deep within that it wasn't good. This party, that I should have been so excited to perform at, was going to be one of the longest nights of my life.

The night ended up being a huge success and the party went on till all hours of the morning. I was paid over two thousand dollars for that event, and it successfully distracted my mind from my toilet incident.

The next day, I went to the toilet three times and there was no blood. I felt relieved; it was a passing thing, a virus, I said to myself. That Sunday was probably the most alive I had felt in years. I was talking and cracking jokes with my family just like old times; I was so happy I wondered whether my parents might have thought I had taken drugs the night before.

Looking back, I sometimes see that day as the calm before the storm— the little window life gives you to enjoy, before it turns your world upside down into a thousand puzzle pieces. Pieces of a puzzle that go missing, that don't come back to the box for you to put together. With this particular puzzle, you have to find, create and mould that puzzle to suit yourself and your way of living. But only a lucky few get to complete this puzzle and display it in their homes as a symbol of triumph, a reminder of the hardship you went through to put that puzzle together.

The thing was, I wasn't a puzzle maker. I was an artist; I painted and illustrated. I wasn't interested in puzzles at all! And now I was to embark on a form of creativity and self-development that would see the final artwork hanging on my wall made entirely out of gold—so rare it would need an army to protect it around the clock. This level of achievement earned me a Master's degree from The University of Life. But was I ready?

Chapter 7

Painting on Thin Ice

Matt, what are you doing home, are you okay?

Monday morning had arrived and I had slept in. Mum came rushing into my room as it hit eight o'clock, my starting time. I knew straightaway I was going to get an earful from the boss. If I went in late, I would cop it for not being on time; if I didn't go in, I would cop it the next day for taking time off. I instantly felt sick at the thought of going to work, especially after the emotional roller-coaster of a weekend I'd just had.

'Mum, can you please ring the boss and tell him I am sick? Tell him I've been up all night and am at the doctors now and won't be in.' Sure, I wasn't at the doctors but I did feel sick enough not to go into work and be abused one way or the other. Luckily for me, my mother never asked too many questions. I gave her the boss' number and she rang for me. 'When I rang him, he sounded a bit grumpy,' she said. *Try dealing with it on a daily basis*, I thought to myself and I went back to sleep.

I didn't sleep in for long and got out of bed only an hour later. I sat with Mum and we had breakfast together. My mother and I are rather close and usually talk about everything together, well most things. But a mother's intuition can never be questioned; you can't see it but you know it's there.

'Matt, what's wrong? You seem quiet,' was all that was needed to set me off. My family and I are very emotional people, sometimes too much so. Another unwanted quality we have is that we suppress our emotions which ends up one of two ways: angry rage or emotional breakdown. That morning, it was an emotional breakdown for me.

I don't know what happened; it was as though something had taken over my body. I broke down with the shakes and started to cry. Now when I say the shakes, my body trembled, my faced turned blue and I was stone cold. My mother panicked and automatically went to find the thickest blanket to cover me.

It did nothing; I was wrapped in a blanket, still shaking as though naked in the snow. I could see Mum panicking even further, as she continued to gather blankets and fill hot water bottles.

After ten minutes of her running around the house trying to stabilise my shakes, I ended up with three thick blankets wrapped around me, a beanie, socks, and cradled two steaming hot water bottles. As she went to call my father, not knowing what to do next, it was as though an angel had passed through and given me a free pass. The shakes disappeared, my crying stopped and I was standing as though supported by my guardian angels.

'Matt, what the hell just happened?' my mother screamed. 'I don't know Mum, I'm going to lie down,' and I did. I went straight back to bed, as though what had happened was something out of a dream. Except this wasn't a dream; what had happened was real and it was the beginning of a journey to a realm that would get more and more unrealistic to this physical world and to the non-believers of the unknown and untaught.

I slept for a good three hours. There was total silence in the house; I'm sure my mother was still trying to digest what had happened. I got out of bed a few hours later and walked out to see her watching TV. But there was nothing on the screen, she was just staring at it with a look of fear in her eyes.

Our family the four of us, have always been quite healthy; apart from the odd weak stomach situation, no-one had ever been to hospital, developed a disease, nothing. So my little experience was something that my mother wasn't familiar with and it definitely instilled fear into her. I sat next to her on the couch and turned the TV on. I just sat beside her for the next four hours until my father came home; not a word was spoken between the two of us.

I was in the bathroom when my father came home. It was still relatively quiet; I didn't know what to expect, to be honest. I wasn't thinking too much about what had happened earlier, I had left it behind me. But my mother and father would not let it go that easily, as I am sure no parent would.

I finished with the toilet and walked out to see my mother and father sitting at the table. I knew they wanted to talk as my parents never sat at the table, especially that early in the day. My father's routine, still to this day, is he'd come home, my mother would make him a cup of tea and they would sit and watch their favourite show until it was time to prepare dinner. 'Matt, what's wrong?' my father asked in his quiet, deep voice, with a look of concern. 'Nothing,' I replied.

Now let's stop for a minute … this is an all too familiar situation with many of us in today's society. How many times have you been involved in a situation where you want to say something so badly it feels as though it's literally sitting on your tongue ready to skydive out of your mouth? As you're about to jump, you either don't at all or redirect and say something which has no relation to what you had intended to say.

Well, this was one of those situations. When my father asked what was wrong I wanted to let loose; I wanted to tell him about the constant abuse from work and that it wasn't my fault. I wanted to tell him that

I hated living, I hated work because of the environment. I wanted to tell him about the health scare. I wanted to tell him that I wanted to DJ full-time and I could make more money in three days as a DJ then I would as a sign-writer in a month. And I wanted to tell him that I needed to quit my day job now!

But all that came out was, 'Nothing Dad, I'm fine, just tired.' My father knew there was something wrong but my parents are not pushy people and let the situation be. I went back to my room and started to draw, something I hadn't done for a while, and felt good just expressing my pain and soul on that piece of paper.

I remember crying myself to sleep that night, the hardest I had ever cried. I was scared to go into work the next day and I was worried about my health. First I had passed blood when I went to the toilet and now I had broken out into some sort of cold spasm. I thought I had a tumour or something. I probably had only three hours of sleep that night and, before I knew it, I was on my way to work, expecting to be belted or hung from the top of our factory unit.

'Oh, look who it is, Snifter! Enjoy your long weekend while we were out in the sun putting your signs up?' My signs? What was the boss' son on about; since when did they become my signs? 'Sorry, I wasn't well yesterday.' 'Sure thing, maybe if you stopped DJ'ing on a weekend you could put more effort in here.' The boss' son continued to ramble on. I zoned out and went upstairs to gather my usual day's work log from the boss.

'What's on for me today boss?' I asked. There was no answer, he just continued to work on the computer screen as though I didn't exist. So I asked again, 'What did you want me to start with this morning?' in a somewhat louder voice, thinking to myself that I wasn't loud enough the first time.

'Do you know how much money you cost me yesterday from your day off?' There it was, I knew he wouldn't let it slip. 'Sorry, I wasn't well' I replied, in my fearful mouse-like voice. 'I don't care how you were feeling; we have work to do and I had a big job on yesterday that had to be done. I had to spend extra money hiring outside sign-writers to get it finished, now I am at a loss.'

By this time he had risen from his chair in front of his computer and was standing an inch away from my face, teeth clenched and screaming at me. Then bang, there it was, that sharp pain in my stomach resurfaced.

He continued his verbal rage for the next five minutes, ending with 'Get out of my sight!' So I made my way downstairs and just hovered, waiting for my orders. When these situations happened, I usually started cleaning the brushes in turpentine. To this day, when I smell turpentine, it instantly reminds me of working there and brings up memories of my past.

The boss' son was singing and dancing as per usual, not talking to me. To be honest, it was as though he was happy that I was copping it from his father; it was probably taking the heat off him and that's why he was so chirpy.

I felt my insides burning from a combination of rage, anger and a whole lot of other negative emotions. I felt it building quickly; my ears were red hot, the pain in my stomach increased and I started to sweat.

'Hey Snifter, grab some scissors and come with me,' the boss' son ordered. I thought to myself, *Please God, take us into a dark place so I can stab him and make it look like an accident.* But that was no act of God, just pure evil and angry thoughts.

We headed out to the front of the building complex where we worked. Now I haven't mentioned that my boss was a very wealthy individual; we worked in a complex that housed seven factory units and he owned them all. He also owned another twelve down the road, where he often sent me to weed the gardens.

We headed to the front of the building and he pointed straight up to the sky. 'See the Australian flag? It's old, here's the new one, change it!' This flag was right on top of the building, two storeys high. 'How am I supposed to reach it?' I asked. 'What, we don't have ladders, you dope? Get the biggest one and climb, you girl!'

Once again I was being forced to risk my life. They knew they could push me as I'd had the previous day off, so I was most likely not going to object and fight back out of fear.

Well, they were partly right. The boss' son headed back into the factory to continue his job and I stayed out the front and looked up at this flag I was supposed to change. It was so high I couldn't even see it because the sun was shining directly in my eyes.

Panic mode kicked in; what was I going to do? I had no energy to begin with, after the weekend that had just passed. I was drained emotionally and the two people who were supposed to have a duty of care in my workplace were not making life any easier. If there was ever a situation where lateral thinking was needed, this was it.

So I headed back into the factory and continued to clean the brushes. 'Oi! What the hell are you doing, why isn't the flag up?' The boss' son had walked over to where I was, shoving the flag into my chest. 'I don't get paid to change flags and risk my life,' I said. 'What did you say?' he replied angrily. It took my all not to belt that guy; my heart was beating out of my chest and I saw red. **'I said that I don't get paid to change flags and risk my life!'** I yelled back.

I finally did it; I stood up for myself. I yelled back to his face and shoved the flag right back into his chest. This was definitely fight mode for me;

I was threatened and developed superhuman powers. The boss' son flew back at least four steps from my retaliation push.

Before he had time to react I pulled out my phone, walking out of the factory and up the street. Now I don't know why I did what I did. I should have got in my car and driven off, but instead I called my brother.

At that time, my brother was a sales manager and worked an hour away from where I was. At that time of the day in Sydney traffic, he would have taken at least two hours to reach me. I remember screaming on the phone, telling him what had happened and bawling my eyes out. 'Matt, go back to the warehouse, pack your toolbox and go home,' was all my brother had said to me, then hung up the phone.

I took some time to control my breathing and gather my thoughts and emotions. By this time, I realised I been walking away from the factory warehouse for nearly half an hour. I wondered how many people had heard me screaming, as I walked past their place of work.

I made my way back to the factory to grab my personal belongings. As I approached I saw two cars parked oddly, as though they were blocking the driveway. Someone had jumped out of the car quickly or perhaps had broken down and was waiting for a tow truck.

Then I recognised that they were my brother and father's cars. Somehow, in the time since I had hung up the phone, my brother had called my father, explained the situation, and they'd both made it to my workplace in record time.

I started to run, in case there was an all-in brawl. This time I wasn't going to hold back, especially with my family involved. All I could hear was swearing and yelling, coming from the boss' office.

My father was holding my brother back, as he was about to take out the big tough boss, who sat quietly with his head down at his desk, his son standing behind him. They knew they had skated on thin ice for far too long and that this was their iceberg ready to take them to the bottom of their ocean.

I walked in and didn't say a word. As soon as I knew my brother and father were okay and had the upper hand I just stood there and watched, ready to attack and defend my family, if these two abusers had something dirty up their sleeves.

My father eventually had to restrain my brother and steer him away from the boss and his son. The last thing I heard my brother say to my boss, pointing at him in rage was, 'Would you allow someone to treat your son like that?' Then he walked off, pushing every paper off the table as he looked at me saying, 'Matt, let's go.'

I didn't immediately follow, as my father was still in the office. He walked up to my boss and said, 'No-one treats my son like this; you will be hearing from me!' Then he walked towards me, telling me to gather my belongings and leave.

That was my last day as a sign-writer. When we returned home that afternoon, I broke down and told my parents and my brother about the abuse I'd copped throughout the years. I told them that I'd kept it a secret because I was frightened that they would think it was my fault and I was scared of my boss.

We all cried that night, we all held each other, and there was a small sense of relief that I wouldn't have to go back to work in that hellhole ever again.

For the next two weeks I didn't do much. I stayed home with my mum. Not much was spoken and each day I would see my father on the phone after work. He handed me papers to sign every now and then; I had no idea what I was signing, but I was signing.

About a month later, I received a confidential envelope in the mail. It was my trade certificate; I was now a fully qualified sign-writer.

Receiving such a qualification should have filled me and my family with pride. But no positive feelings ran through my veins at all, not one ounce. I didn't care, I wanted to rip up that piece of paper, it meant nothing to me. All it did was remind me of the pain and the physical and mental scars I was left with.

I put the certificate on the mantelpiece and returned to my room, continuing to draw as I did most days. When my father returned from work that day he knocked on my door ever so gently, as I was still on edge at that time. Most nights I would scream multiple times during my sleep, so my parents had become wary about me. It could not have been easy for them.

'So you're a tradesman now, congratulations!' I didn't reply; I wondered how and why I had become a tradesman, as I hadn't completed the full four-year apprenticeship. I had served a total of three and a half years. But my curiosity got the better of me and I asked my father how it had come to be. 'Dad, how did I become fully qualified, when I didn't complete the time?' My father explained that all of those phone calls that I'd heard him make for the past two months had been to the board of apprenticeships, explaining my situation. Because I had worked so much unpaid overtime, I had completed the practical hours needed to become a tradesman. That's how and why I could be released.

Well my curiosity had been satisfied but that hadn't changed my feelings. I continued to draw, while my father stayed sitting on my bed behind my desk. I turned and looked at him ... 'What?' I asked. He told me that he had also called WorkCover and told them how I'd been working at illegal heights without a choice, so they had started an investigation into my former boss.

Well, as the old saying goes, the fat lady sang and the song was sung. My father's next words really hit home: 'Matt, WorkCover called me back today. Thanks to my call and their investigations, they have enough evidence to charge your boss with illegal practice and he is facing jail time.' I could not believe it! I didn't care that he was going to jail or that he was going to pay for his sins. What was most satisfying was that the proof was there and had been illustrated to me in stone. I wasn't the one causing trouble in my work place. An outside authority had proved it was not my doing. That to me was the most satisfying thing, more than my trade certificate.

I gave my father a hug, fought back tears, as did he, and continued to draw.

That day was bittersweet for me, It was a triumph, knowing that an evil person, someone who had held a gun to my soul for almost four years, was about to face the consequences. That was a great feeling. At the same time, I didn't know it but I had been emotionally scarred. I had been scarred so deeply within that when it came to the surface it would affect more than my outside world. It would eat into my insides, like termites eat into wood. This would introduce me to a form of abuse that was the most aggressive of all: abuse from within.

Chapter 8

The Art of Turntablism

What's on the gig guide for this weekend, son?

My father asked every Tuesday afternoon when he returned from work. He always gave me Monday to recover from my heavy weekend DJ schedule.

After the whole sign-writing experience, I would not even think of going to work for anyone else. I focused all of my energy on what I knew best, my DJ career, and I gave it my all.

I continued to DJ on weekends, mostly weddings and corporate events, but I hungered for more. I was a great DJ—there wasn't a party I couldn't rock. Hell, I would even get people up at a christening!

I set my sights on the big time, nightclub work. Nightclub DJ'ing was where it was at; you were centre of attention with your name in lights and you could make some serious income, if your name was well-known.

I knew that's where I wanted to be but wasn't sure who to contact. Everyone I spoke to in the game made it very clear that only a select few get to play at nightclub level. Only elite DJs performed at that level, which made me want it even more.

I continued to DJ at weekly corporate events. Most finished at midnight, when I would quickly pack up, get changed and make my way into the city to the hottest clubs around.

There was one particular club I had my sights set on, probably the largest club at the time in Sydney playing my style of music. It was situated under the casino and all the top DJs played there; that's where I wanted to be.

Every Saturday night I would head to that club after my corporate gig. I'd arrive around one o'clock in the morning, which was when most clubs were just getting started. For the first two months or so I would simply wait in line, pay my entrance fee and literally find a spot inside the club. I'd zone everything out—the drugs, the women, the alcohol—and focus all of my energy on the DJ.

At that time, I was subconsciously scouting my scene; I was preparing mentally and studying the art of turntablism. I would listen to each DJ; there was a different one every hour. I would study the crowd, who reacted differently to each DJ and each song that was dropped. There was a real science to this and I wanted to be the Einstein of DJ'ing.

Every Saturday I would stay at the club until around three o'clock in the morning. By that time, the club would start to die down. I was on pins and needles wanting to get up on stage to express my soul through those turntables. I would rush home in the early hours of Sunday morning, wide-awake and full of excitement. I'd rush straight to my room and practise what I had witnessed just a few hours earlier at the club.

I can remember closing my eyes and visualising me in front of that crowd, DJ'ing the main set. I would do that almost every time I practised. I didn't realise it then, but 'visualisation becoming actualisation' became the norm for me later in my life, and continues in my work today.

I would practise until I fell asleep at the turntables. My practice sessions were never loud. I didn't need to play the music through my speakers, just through my headphones, so there was never any worry about waking up my parents.

Every Sunday morning my father would come to my room to check on me. I would have records spread out everywhere and I would be lying in my bed, wearing clothes from the night before. I can't imagine what it looked like.

I look back now and wonder what was going on in my parents' minds. I can honestly say that in my many years of DJ'ing, with the extensive travel I was involved in at my peak and the number of hours I worked, I never took a drug or even drank alcohol. That's very hard to believe for many, but let me illustrate and explain further.

There's an old saying: *You never work a day in your life, when you love what you do.* Well, I loved to DJ; I would have married it if I could! I was controlling hundreds of people on a dance floor with my fingers and I can't express the true feeling of joy I was in when I was in my element as a DJ. The only words that could possibly describe the feeling would be 'complete euphoria'.

It was a Tuesday morning, the time when I'd organise my weekly diary. By that time, I had started my own small entertainment company, leasing out DJs to various venues across Sydney. I would receive a commission from each DJ.

That was my first taste of earning money while sleeping—passive income, so to speak. To be honest, the entire set-up of that business came naturally; I just knew what to do and when to do it.

That particular week, I didn't personally have a gig booked for the Saturday. In hindsight, I should have taken the night off to enjoy myself and reap the benefit of having more than twenty DJs out working for me. But instantly I thought what a perfect opportunity it was to get to the club early, find out who the promoter was, hand them my demo and persuade them to give me a shot. I felt a rush of excitement and poured all my energy that week into producing a crisp, sharp mixtape, to stimulate the hearing senses of the promoters, who would then want me to play at their club.

Saturday night finally arrived. It was eight o'clock and the club opened at ten. 'Aren't you at work tonight, Matt?' my father asked, as I was not dressed in my usual formal attire and I'd usually be out of the house and at work by that time. 'Dad, I'm off to become famous tonight, so you better ask for my autograph now, champ!' I was, and still am, very close to my father. I joke with him a lot. He probably didn't understand half of the things that would come out of my mouth, but I was smiling and I think that's all he cared about.

I high fived my father, left home and was on my way to the casino, listening to my mix tape the whole way. Now I am not an egoist but that mixtape was pretty good; I could hardly find fault with it. I was pumped! If I was happy with it, there was no way the promoter wouldn't be so he'd hire me on the spot. This night was going to be a game changer!

I entered the casino car park. As usual it was full, especially that late at night. Luckily I knew back streets where some quick access street parking would be, so I quickly whipped around into my secret spot and landed a car space three metres from the club entrance. This night was panning out perfectly.

I was about half an hour early, which would give me enough time to casually weed out the promoter, then present myself and explain my goals and how I could be best implemented into their club. I checked out how I looked in my rear vision mirror, fixed my clothes and was off. There was always a bunch of people standing outside any club, especially in Sydney, before the doors opened. Security guards, girls whose role I'd never really understood, the clipboard person who always lived in ego, and a bunch of other people standing around trying to look important.

'Excuse me, I am looking for the promoter.' Then, 'I'm the promoter, is there a problem?' This was it, the guy I needed, the decision–maker, so it all came down to this moment. I was standing in front of the hottest club in Sydney, in front of the guy that called the shots, about to ask if I could become a part of his crew. My heart was in my mouth.

'Hi I'm Matt, I come here each week. I'm a DJ and would love to play here.' Not the best opening pitch, but that's the sentence I seem to have put together. 'Have you got a demo?' 'Sure, here you go.' I swiftly handed him my freshly-made CD. 'Thanks, leave it with me.' Then he walked off. That was it, after a week of mental preparation while producing the mixtape, with a million scenarios running through my head on how and what to say, this guy has grabbed my CD, handed it to one of the wannabe promoters and walked off.

I didn't know what to do; I was standing at the front of the club in shock. At one point I caught myself with my mouth hanging open and I shut it instantly. I walked away in a cloud of confusion. It was not what I had expected and, the worst part was, he didn't even seem interested. He had just palmed off my CD and probably had no intention of listening to the mixtape I'd put together just for him.

I drove home that night with the radio down; I wasn't angry or upset, I was just confused. Maybe the club scene was hard to get into and everyone in the industry was right. Maybe it was only for the elite and perhaps it wasn't part of my path to become a major club scene DJ.

I arrived home before midnight on that Saturday night, the earliest in a while. My father woke up and instantly thought something was wrong. I confirmed everything was fine and went straight to bed, trying to re-enact that night's events in my mind, to pinpoint any vital or positive information I may have missed. I found nothing and fell asleep, with a million scenarios playing in my head.

Next morning, I woke up quite refreshed. It was the best sleep I'd had in months, as I was home early the night before. For some reason, the club incident was not on my mind and I didn't allow it to go there, which was rare for me. Most things eat at me until they affect me healthwise or in some other crippling way.

Now that particular mindset of letting things go is very important. At that time, life was about to teach me a very valuable lesson: to allow things and events to grow and happen organically in life, to let yourself go and allow the angels to guide you.

Now this doesn't mean sitting at home on the couch and waiting for something to happen. That's nonsense, and is just an excuse for those who are lazy and want life handed to them. What it means is that patience is a very important tool to master; to this day I still have not mastered it. To be honest, I don't think I ever will; but what I have learnt is how to recognise a situation that requires patience and let the universe work its magic.

You see, that Sunday morning I woke up feeling happy which was unexpected, considering what had happened the night before. But on this particular day I felt at peace. This was the universe telling me to allow the angels to work behind the scenes, placing little deposits or signs in my mind or along my physical path for me to follow, allowing things to happen when they were meant to happen, without being forced.

For the next two months I continued to work within the corporate scene. I employed a further fifteen DJs and I was personally booked four nights a week. I stopped going to the club every Saturday night; I didn't even think about it. I was focused on my clients, my team and my business. I was content with the success I was having and had massive plans for business expansion.

Another successful week in my gig guide was ahead; my team was unstoppable. It was Tuesday morning and I was about to check my emails when my phone rang. It was a number I wasn't familiar with; I usually never answer unknown phone numbers. But sometimes the universe wants an event to happen. Whether you believe in fate or luck, on this particular day I found myself picking up that phone call. 'Matt speaking.' If I didn't know who was on the other end of the line I always answered in a deep, scary voice, hoping I would intimidate the other person, in case it was someone I didn't want to speak to.

It was a girl's voice, softly spoken, but her words were loud and clear: 'Hi Matt, I am calling on behalf of the club promoter under the casino, who you dropped your demo off to a short while ago. He's had a chance to listen to it and was very impressed and wondered if you were available to do an opening set this Saturday from ten till midnight?'

I went blank, I didn't say a word and even dropped the phone only to hear, 'Matt hello, are you there?' I quickly picked up the phone and put my confident voice on replying, 'I do apologise, I am having problems with the line. Can you bear with me while I check my diary?'

Now even if I had been booked to DJ the Pope's party at the Vatican, I was not giving up the opportunity to DJ at this club. After thirty seconds of flicking through my diary, making sure the girl at the other end could hear me, I replied, 'Yeah look, I have a gig on that night but I can shift it onto one of my team members and I would love to trial at your club. Do I need to bring anything?' 'That's great Matt, all you need to bring is your music and turn up half an hour prior to your set as you are opening, to do a sound check and ensure all the equipment is working fine. If you don't have any more questions, we will see you then.'

I didn't have any questions; I didn't even ask what the pay was; I would have played for free. I calmly replied with 'Thank you for the opportunity and see you on Saturday night,' and hung up the phone.

This is a perfect illustration of an organically-grown event that blossomed at the time it needed to. I could have hounded the promoter at the club every week, showing enthusiasm and wanting to know what he thought of my mixtape and whether I had a shot at performing at the club. That would have achieved one thing: frustrating and annoying him. So he'd instantly dismiss my CD, no matter how good it was. If someone doesn't like you as a person, you simply will not get what you have set out to achieve; there are many behind you waiting in line, ready to take your place.

That Tuesday morning after the phone call, I can remember sitting at my desk, holding my phone in my hand and staring at my computer screen, seeing only a blur. My mother was sitting on the couch having her morning hot lemon tea. I yelled out with the biggest roar of excitement and jumped up and down, as though I had just one a million dollars. When I'd explained the entire situation, my mother joined in my dance of joy.

I can distinctly remember the warm fuzzy feeling that raced through my body that day. It was a feeling of achievement, as though I finally meant something in this world. I was being recognised for my skills and talents and not being abused in any way. Let me tell you, no amount of money can instil that form of natural high within every cell of your body. That day I was inspired.

I did not leave my room all week; I practised every hour I was awake. My mother brought meals to my room. I was on a mission, after all of those weeks studying the DJs at the club: what they played, how they mixed each track and what tricks they implemented. I was preparing for the most important two-hour audition and I wouldn't allow anything to get in my way.

Saturday morning had arrived. Oh man, I was pumped! I didn't practise much that day as I wanted to walk in fresh. I filled the day with things that made me happy. I sketched a lot, watched a few movies (a passion of mine to this day), and spent time with the family dog.

Before I knew it, it was time to get ready. I remember having a shower that night feeling at peace, not nervous. It was as though I had been doing this for years. Added to that, I had more than thirty DJs scattered all over Sydney that night working for me, so I should have been a little worried, but I wasn't.

I was about to embark on something people had told me was impossible, that DJs in the game for over fifteen years had never been given a chance at. But here I was, getting dressed and packing my records, about to audition against all odds.

I gave my parents a kiss and a hug and both wished me luck. But I knew this was the universe's game plan and my fate. I had this, it was written. I gave them a smile and made my way to the club.

That night happened as though the angels had produced a perfectly outlined piece of art. All I had to do was fill in the lines with the colours that would best appeal to the viewing eye.

There was no traffic heading in, unheard of on a Saturday night in the city, so I arrived an hour early and found parking right outside the club. I headed to the front of the club and saw the same group of people as on the night I handed in my demo CD. But this time I wasn't handing in a demo, I **was** the demo, and I was about to show these people what that mixtape sounded like live.

'Matt, how are you? Welcome, let me show you your tools for the next two hours.' I was greeted by the same promoter who had palmed off my CD a mere two months ago. He was now welcoming me into his home so to speak, as though I was his best friend.

We made our way through the club. It had two rooms, one was off to the right and only housed about a hundred people and then there was my room, the main room, which held seven hundred people at full capacity, the biggest club in Sydney at that time.

As we made our way to the DJ booth, waiters, waitresses and workers were preparing the club for a big night ahead. They didn't know who I was, but they had a look painted on their faces as if to say, 'Who is this guy? He must be important, as he is with the club promoter.' I was greeted with smiles and winks and felt like a superstar. And the club wasn't even open for business yet.

'Are you familiar with this set-up?' It was exactly what I had at home, two turntables and a mixer, even the exact same mixer I worked with at home, which eased the few nerves I had. 'Absolutely!' I replied. 'Great, put a record on and let's test the sound and make sure everything is in working order.' Everything worked fine, I got the thumbs up from the promoter and he left me to set up my records and DJ booth.

I can remember sitting there about ten minutes before the club opened. The room was dark, I was on stage and the disco lights were on, as though they had started the party already. I looked up, smiled and said 'Thank you'. I was giving thanks to the higher source, for allowing me to be at that point and share my passion with people who appreciated what I did. I was ready to impress the promoter of the biggest club in Sydney.

'Now Matt, we are about to open doors when you're ready. Just play like you did on your mixtape and impress the crowd, as you did me.' That short inspirational speech from the promoter was the last I saw of him for my entire set. I put the needle on my first record, placed my headphones on and that entire week's worth of practice in my bedroom was about to become a reality. I was about to play to a different crowd; these weren't corporates, this wasn't a 21st birthday with family and friends, this was a booty shaking, no rules club! They wanted to dance and hear from the best of the best, and I was not going to disappoint.

For the first half hour there weren't many people in the club. That didn't worry me too much as I was familiar with the club scene; I knew how the system worked. Build the line up outside so it looks busy inside, in order to build an even bigger entry line and slowly allow people in. So I continued to spin, everything was flowing, all of my mixes were great. I was playing everything at the right tempo, no club hits played prematurely, and the few people that were in the club got bopping.

I was in between mixes; I can remember I was sampling one track into the next, playing and trying a few little tricks. I was in my own world; this was the art of turntablism at its best. I caught myself smiling, having a ball, and then I brought the next track in. As I went to take the previous track off to put the next record on, I looked up. There were at least a hundred people dancing; within the change of a track, the dance floor had begun to fill.

I was taken aback. I had been playing to an empty club for the last forty minutes and now there were a hundred people dancing to my sounds and ninety percent were women. Now even though I had been DJ'ing for years and played every event you could think of, no event meant more than this night. To be honest, I wasn't prepared mentally for that dance floor to be packed so early, especially when I was the driver of the music.

Through the grapevine, I had heard that clubs don't get started until midnight and the opening DJ always played to the staff. I was fine with that, especially for my trial, it was just a foot in the door. But on this night it was different, and now I had to make every track count.

A club gig is very different to a structured corporate event. A club gig is basically raw; if the club goers do not like what you're playing, you will lose the dance floor or, even worse, they will throw bottles at you. All is being witnessed by the promoter and, if you don't get it right the first time, there are thousands of DJs waiting to replace you.

As soon as I realised I had connected with the crowd through my music selection, I had to ensure that every track that followed counted. So I changed the set that I practised so intensely the week before, and let the crowd guide me through their energy.

The next hour and a half saw the dance floor never empty. Every track I played tickled the crowd and, with each drop and mix of a song, you heard a cheer from the crowd, which only excited me further. I had that club rocking and I didn't want it to end. I could tell my set was about to finish as the next DJ had arrived, made his way through the rocking crowd with his crate of records, and jumped on stage behind me. 'Man, I have never seen the club rocking as early as this before!' he screamed in my ear

I reached the last ten minutes of my set and we began to change over turntable needles, leading me into my last track. I remember playing that last track of the two-hour audition, feeling as though I was playing at my own farewell party.

I remember looking at the crowd, a sea of hands in the air, smiles lighting up the dance floor, people were bumping and grinding. Now I was about to hand over to the next DJ, only hoping the promoter saw that it was me who'd set the tone for the remainder of the night, not this guy.

I stayed around for the next hour to wind down and listen to this DJ, to see how I compared. To be honest, I was so much more skilled than he was and, during that hour, the dance floor had patches of emptiness. I finally grabbed my crates of records, high fived the DJ, then walked out.

The girl I'd spoken to on the phone was at the club entrance. She looked busy and a bit flustered. I didn't know what to do; I wasn't sure what the process was. Did I invoice them? Should I say thanks? I couldn't even see the promoter. She reached into the till, lifted the cash tray and handed me an envelope with my name on it. She said thanks, gave me a hug and that was it.

It was all over, the club gig that everyone in the industry said I couldn't do. I couldn't be happier with what I had produced, but I wasn't sure what the next move was.

I eventually made my way home that night and found myself sitting on my bed, just thinking of my set that night and what I had just experienced. My phone vibrated and a message popped up from the promoter: *Sorry I missed you, busy night, speak soon.* That was it; no feedback on my set, negative or positive, just neutral. Then I remembered the envelope with my name on it.

I opened my zipped-up jacket pocket and took out the envelope, not sure what I would find. I was not expecting to be paid for my trial but there it was ... five hundred dollars in cash ... for just two hours' work. I could not believe it. I was used to getting paid a couple of hundred more for a corporate gig but I had to lug around almost $50,000 worth of equipment to each event, so this was unbelievable.

I stared in awe at the pile of cash in my hand and wanted that night to happen every week. The money was just an added bonus and an unexpected one at that. I thought, *If this is what an opening set DJ gets paid, what do the elite get?* That envelope changed everything for me; it opened my eyes to what could be earned in the same business, doing less work. I wanted more of the pie I had just tasted.

Next Monday came quickly. I had a huge week ahead of private gigs, so the club gig was a little to the back of my mind. I was filtering through my emails when I came across one that stood out from the rest. I instantly thought it was a bridezilla, wanting to change something for her wedding that weekend. But to my surprise, the email was from the club promoter. It was from his personal email address and simply read: *Lunch today?*

A thousand scenarios raced through my mind, both positive and negative, and I did what any man would do and with all my ego replied: *Sure, where and when?*

Luckily it was a place I was familiar with. As he hadn't given me much notice, I jumped in the shower and made my way to the restaurant. The promoter was already sitting at a table close to a window with his back facing me. It felt like a meeting with the mafia; meeting someone at a quiet restaurant and sitting in a booth out of sight of most passers-by.

'Hey sorry I'm late, parking was a nightmare.' It wasn't, but I needed to break the ice and calm my nerves a little. 'That's fine, I've just arrived.' We began to browse the menu. I'm sure he was hungry, but I wasn't. I was anxious but still ordered anyway, as I didn't want to be rude. I ordered a hamburger with fries and sat back, ready to receive my marching orders or praise.

'Matt, I have been in this game a long time and have been in charge of some of the largest nightclubs in this country. I need to be honest with you.' Here it was, he was about to lay into me, I was sure of it. 'Matt, no DJ has ever been able to fill a dance floor that early in the night and hold them there for the entire set the way you did.'

Wait, what did this guy just say? He went on to tell me that DJs who have been in the game for ten years couldn't achieve what I did that night, especially with that much execution and passion. Apparently I'd had the club staff and his own staff talking for days after.

I was overwhelmed and didn't know how to reply. I didn't say anything, I just smiled. Then out of nowhere he followed with the words that would change not only that moment in time for me, they would change the face of DJ'ing in Sydney and how everyone experienced it, both patrons and workers. A new set of rules were about to be written and I was holding the pen.

'Matt, I am impressed. Guys like you come around very rarely, so I want to offer you a weekly residency at the club. We will situate you in the same set, the first two hours each Saturday, and then shift you into the main set when you get to know the crowd more. Between you and I, I am about to open three more clubs that I want you to be a part of. What do you think?'

What did I think; was this guy serious? I had just been offered a weekly position at the hottest night spot in Sydney. He had just stated that I was more skilled than DJs he had worked with for over ten years; and he'd shared his future business plans with me, wanting me to be a part of them.

Where do I sign? I wanted to shout. But I took two deep breaths and said, 'That sounds great; when would you see me starting?' 'This Saturday!' And with perfect timing our lunch arrived and he was into it, as though it was his first meal in weeks.

Not much was spoken for the next twenty minutes or so. He was busy devouring his lunch and I was eating my fries one by one. I'm surprised I didn't choke; I don't think I was even chewing; I was still digesting what just had happened.

When our meals were finished he shook my hand, paid the bill and said, 'I will have my assistant email you all of the details; welcome to the team, big things for you ahead!' and walked off. I was left sitting at the table with three quarters of my lunch still on my plate and a smile from ear to ear. In a matter of an hour. the course of my life had changed and for the good. Starting that weekend, I was a resident DJ at the club I had handed my demo tape to, just two months before.

I was about to show the world what I was made of and share my passion with a businessman and promoter who actually appreciated me for what I did. That was the greatest personal drug of achievement one could have.

I arrived home and floated back to reality, remembering the gigs for the coming weekend that I had to organise. I had committed to many corporate events and now could not be a part of them. I was embarking on my new career: nightclub work.

So I took a few hours to think about the best way to approach the situation and came up with the perfect solution. Each booked event was a corporate gig and had no relation to one another. I would simply continue to organise the events as per usual, but not take on any further Saturday work. Every Thursday before a corporate event I would call the client with a fake sick voice, say I was sorry but I had the flu and didn't want to show up to their wedding or function sick. So I would send one of my professional protégés in my place. Nine times out of ten there was no issue.

I was a great problem–solver. Sure, it wasn't totally honest, but I wasn't going to lose the opportunity with the nightclub or lose the business I had built up. And I did continue to DJ at corporate events during the week and on Sundays.

All of my energy and focus were on one thing and one thing only: becoming the greatest DJ Sydney had ever known. I continued to impress the promoter, keeping me fresh in his mind whenever he opened a new club.

Everything I had envisioned was about to come to fruition, bigger than I ever expected. There was just one element I didn't plan for; really, I don't think anyone ever plans for such a thing. But this element would change the game even more and open up a whole new world for me, a world that I needed to experience. I was about to be tested in more ways than one with a handbook of life lessons.

Chapter 9

When Colours Collide

Matt, are you hungry? Let's go and grab something to eat.

I'd had almost a year of DJ'ing at an elite level. My corporate entertainment company was now being operated by an Operations Manager, who I'd hired to oversee everything and just send me a weekly review by email. This allowed me to concentrate on building myself up as a brand in the nightclub scene, and have the occasional midweek lunch with friends who worked night shifts.

I now had my pick of what sets I wanted to play and which clubs I wanted to play at. Most nights I played at four clubs, one hour at each. This particular Saturday night I was doing the graveyard shift, two o'clock till close, which was usually about three thirty in the morning. I had played three earlier sets so I was pretty tired, but I was set to make $2,000 that night, so I wasn't really complaining. Not to mention the commissions from my working DJs serving my corporate entertainment company.

At the end of the last set you would always see the drunks, the emotional ones, and the individuals requesting you to play one more song— begging you to play it as though that one last song would change their life.

When the lights turned on, a huge layer of smoke, from a combination of cigarettes and multiple smoke machines, lay over the room. My ears would ring, something I just became accustomed to, and my eyes would sting from a combination of everything.

This particular night would change the way I viewed the world, the way I viewed business and me as a person. The promoter and I had become really close, but never so close that we'd talk about finances. But on this night, a shift happened. He had asked me to help him cash up, which I found quite odd. Technically I was an employee of his, so I thought: *Why would a boss want their employee to see how much money they were making?* But I didn't ask questions and went off to help.

He had already bagged the money so the next job was to carry the cash upstairs to a private room, so he could count it. I thought that's where my job would end. 'Just tip your bag on the desk; we will count it first.' I was wrong; I was about to help this guy count five bags of cash, all paper notes. He handed me elastic bands and told me to sort the notes into piles. Then we would work together, him counting, me writing down the cash amounts.

It took us about forty minutes and my mind was blown; we had counted a total of $45,000. I couldn't believe it! My ringing ears and stinging eyes had disappeared; it was like I'd been introduced to a lifesaving drug.

I wasn't jealous, I was excited. After all, I was making great money from DJ'ing alone and, combined with my own entertainment business, I was probably earning on average $15,000 a week. But this guy was on a whole new level.

'A lot of money, right?' he said. 'Yeah, just a bit' I replied. I didn't know what to say and I didn't want him to think I would rip him off or try to steal from him, so I didn't show my emotions. But in my mind I was dancing in the rain. And the rain in my vision was me throwing the night's earnings in the air from glee! I had a big grin on my face.

'Matt, are you hungry? Let's go grab something to eat.' Now this wasn't anything unusual; when you're in the entertainment industry, especially nightclub work, your diet isn't the best. I never drank alcohol, sure I might have had the occasional drink but that was it; and drugs, never!! The crowd was my drug, my high was their energy, and that never changed throughout my DJ career.

With that said, I did indulge in a combination of lethal drugs, the ones that are legal but aren't promoted as legal drugs, the silent killers. You see, when DJ'ing, you adopt something that I call the 'DJ diet'. This is a diet of fast food, energy drinks, minimal sleep and late night meals. That particular night we were going to a regular of ours, open almost 24/7, a Chinese restaurant located in Chinatown.

The club was located only ten minutes away, so we hopped into the promoter's car and left mine in the car park. Just the promoter and I, we walked into the restaurant and greeted the staff as though they were family. We sat in the corner away from everyone, but positioned so we could see every part of the restaurant.

'Great night, hey Matt?' 'Yeah man, the crowd was pumping.' We indulged in small talk as we skimmed our menus. But we weren't skimming anything, we'd both been to this restaurant numerous times, so we knew those menus inside out. Crispy skin chicken, two large fried rice, salt and pepper king prawns, beef in oyster sauce and spring rolls; a great meal for two at almost four o'clock in the morning, right?

'So, not a bad taking tonight, hey Matt?' He didn't waste any time 'Absolutely.' I kept my answers brief, as I needed to work out where he was going with all of this. *Matt, DJ'ing is great but this is a business and I know you're different. I knew it from the day you dropped your demo off to me—you're that needle in the haystack. So tonight I am going to share some wisdom with you.'*

I had heard and read in various business forums that you need a mentor in business, someone who is older, who has had experience in both failing and winning, and someone who can lead you. This guy fit easily into all of those categories. But as he was in the night life business I was a little anxious about what would come out of his mouth next. Perhaps he was about to ask me to get involved in some illegal activities? I definitely did not want that; I wasn't that kind of person. Even though I enjoyed the freedom and choice that came with money, I still lived by my own moral compass.

'Okay I'm listening,' I replied. 'Matt, you're a great DJ, you do well, and you do well with your corporate business, right?' Wait … was he telling me I was doing well? When did he find out about my corporate DJ supply business? I had never mentioned anything to him. Sure, we were in the same industry but at totally different levels.

By this time, I was fully awake; I sat up in my chair and he had my undivided attention. I needed to know exactly what he was thinking, how much he knew about me as a person, my business, and where he was going with it all. Thankfully I didn't need to panic too much about the information he shared with me over the next two hours, while we both slowly ate meals that could have fed a third world country.

That night he shared some great insights, very intelligent business strategies and elements of his money making structure with me. The best part was that he showed me what was achievable with minimal experience. I would be able to continue DJ'ing and doing anything else I was passionate about.

We finished our meals as the sun rose. I was dropped back to my car, we shook hands and that was that. I made my way home with the radio down, as I did every night after I played. To be honest, it was as though I'd absorbed nothing from that night's meeting.

I arrived home on that Sunday morning at six o'clock. My father was sitting on the couch in his dressing–gown, drinking a cup of tea. He would never say anything to me, just give me a look as if he were thinking: *Really, you're coming home at this time and you're not on drugs?'* I would always give him a smile, as if to say everything was okay.

That week I had a wedding to DJ on the Saturday night. I hadn't played at a wedding in over a year; the only reason I'd taken this gig was because it was for close friends who really wanted me to play at their wedding. I had told the promoter that night at dinner and he was fine about it, as I had given him a week's notice.

Weddings are very chilled gigs; you get to eat five-star meals, get dressed in your best suit and you're home by one o'clock, depending on the location.

I'd had a rather quiet week. I'd had a rare face to face with my Operations Manager, a meeting lasted for about three hours. Then, for the rest of the week, I prepared the songs and met with the bride and groom for the last time, three days prior to the wedding as was standard procedure.

Saturday arrived, a glorious day, not too hot, no wind, no clouds, a perfectly illustrated day for my friends to get married. I attended the church which was local, then made my way back home to load the car, make my way to the venue, set everything up, conduct a sound check, then a leisurely conversation with the owner over multiple coffees.

Over the years I had built up great relationships with the owners of nearly every popular reception house in Sydney. These venues were booked out every weekend. I held the exclusive entertainment contracts for most, so I had continuous work hiring out my DJs and any other form of entertainment they needed.

I was good at running my operation; I had good staff who did their job well. I received no complaints so, in return, I had a great relationship with the owners, which allowed me freedom on many levels.

The guests had started to be seated; it was only a matter of minutes before my first job, playing the entry music and liaising with the MC on the night about introducing the bridal party.

'Are you guys excited? The hard work is done, now it's party time!' I always revved up the bride and groom before they entered. This event was a little different, as the couple and I were close friends, but I still treated them as important clients. 'It's show time guys, I will see you down there, just enjoy your night.'

I was all set up, ready with the entry music. The MC was introducing himself to the guests, setting down the ground rules and about to introduce the bridal party. As per usual, the MC and I were in sync. The bridal party entrance went with a bang, everyone was clapping, dancing, the bridal party were served their first course. I had a seat at the entertainers' table which I found a bit strange as it was my friends' wedding, not a stranger's. But once again, there was a higher source working behind the scenes.

The entertainers' table was always great; it always consisted of the DJ, the MC, a winging camera man and videographer and whoever else was working on the event. I am usually quick to network and hand out cards, but this night I was quiet. I didn't really feel like talking, I was content with sitting and just being.

That night I experienced indirectly what was probably my first moment of knowing. What is 'knowing'? Well, it is when you know something is about to happen in a positive way; you don't know what, when or how, but you just know within that it will. And you hold all of the right tools to handle and embrace whatever that knowing brings to fruition.

I had finished my entree and was sitting back in my chair, as my work didn't really start until after the mains were served, at least an hour away. I sat back with a peaceful smile and looked around the room, seeing people happy, laughing, talking. There was love in the air … was it love, or was it the angels about to place a deposit right in front of me? This time I would recognise it as clearly as someone slapping me in the face with a rolled-up newspaper.

As my eyes scanned the room every thing became blurry. Now I don't mean that as a metaphor, everything was literally blurry, all I could see was a bright light. I rubbed my eyes but still couldn't make out the people on my table. I had no peripheral vision, nothing, there was just a bright light. I started to panic and rubbed my eyes frantically. I felt my way to the table, found my glass of water, dipped my fingers in it and rubbed my eyes, hoping that when I opened them I could see again.

I can't explain or understand what had happened. In one moment I had gone from peacefully gazing around the room to becoming almost blind. Thankfully, after rubbing my eyes in water, my vision started to reappear. I didn't get it back straightaway, it came back gradually, everything was still pixelated but slowly returned to normal.

After about five minutes I had regained my normal sight. I didn't make a scene, just sat there wondering what in the world had happened. As I started to look around again, that bright light was brighter. It was as though someone or something was shining a torch right in my face, wanting me to see whatever it was they were highlighting. I had no choice but to direct my eyes to this ever-so-bright light, and there it was, a candelabra—a candle holder with three branches, that had featured at every wedding I had DJ'd at. For some reason tonight, this half-burnt candle was making its presence known to me.

'Matt, it's time for speeches.' The MC got the speeches underway, which meant it was almost time for dancing. I made my way back to my DJ set-up, putting what had just happened to the back of my mind, allowing me to get on with the night's work.

The night was a great success. The bride and groom didn't stop dancing, the guests had the dance floor covered all night, and the owners of the reception venue were happy with me once again. Once all of the guests had gone, I would normally pack my equipment up slowly, talking to the waiters and cracking jokes, then make my way home.

But tonight was different. 'Matt, let's have a coffee.' The owner invited me upstairs to his office. This was very rare, as he usually left for the night just after mains were served, leaving his staff to lock up. But that night he was on hand, so I found myself about to have a late night coffee with him, a change from Chinese I guess.

Our conversation mainly consisted of how my DJs had been serving him at past events. Then out of nowhere, I found myself saying, 'What's the deal with your candles on the main table? They nearly blinded me tonight; the flame was so bright.' Now I don't know where that came from, but it hurtled out of my mouth as though it was a horse out of the gates. 'Tell me about it, these candles are crap. I tell you what Matt, if you can supply us with something better which wouldn't be hard, we would purchase long-term from you straightaway; there are no reliable candle suppliers in this industry!'

Now if you are an ordinary conformed person, not paying attention to the signs or deposits, the statement that was just made would have flown right over your head. You would agree, finish your coffee, collect your night's wages and leave.

Well, I wasn't a conformed person, and it all added up. The conversation a week prior at the Chinese restaurant with the promoter and the one wedding event I'd DJ'd after so long out of the corporate scene. That light blinding me and being ever so present in my line of sight and, most importantly, one of the elements the promoter had spoken about at our early morning Chinese meal came into alignment.

To go back to the Chinese restaurant, one the elements the promoter had spoken about, which I found myself mechanically scrolling through while sitting in front of the wedding venue owner, was the word 'diversify'.

The promoter had outlined a very important strategic move in business: that no matter how much money you make in one industry and how well you are generating an income from one trade, you need to use that money or a portion of it to invest in other 'sure thing' companies and businesses.

What were 'sure thing' companies and businesses? Ones that you didn't need to use your own money to start, ones that sold things that people needed and came back for, and ones that didn't involve products with a shelf life.

This was a winning lottery ticket and I held the winning numbers. All I had to do was find a supplier for quality candles that fitted the venue's requirements: correct size, burning time and no drip. If I could meet all these requirements and design a way to ship them without using my money, which would lower my risk even more, I was onto something big!

I raced home that night, jumped straight onto the internet, and looked for overseas candle suppliers fitting my requirements. I searched overseas, as I knew they would cost too much to manufacture in Australia. All I knew was that there was a kink in the armour of the wedding reception industry and it was a key part to the night and each event. Candles set the mood, saved electricity and they needed to be replaced for every event, as no bride or groom would want half-burnt candles at their wedding. This was a gold mine at the end of a rainbow; I was about to stumble to the end of that rainbow and collect my pot of gold.

After three weeks of constant back and forth emails to various overseas suppliers and receiving samples, I finally found a company that met my needs. The candles needed to be dripless, scentless and have a burning time of seven hours and this supplier met all of those requirements.

The manufacturer's requirement was that I order five pallets a month minimum, which worked out to be around 25,000 candles. So if I was going to do this, I needed to have guaranteed long-term sales, otherwise it wouldn't work. I would lose a lot financially as well as the trust of the wedding venues, which would hurt my entertainment business.

It was a Wednesday morning, the day to make my way to all of the reception houses that my DJs had worked that past weekend and collect payment. It was unconventional but I was never paid through the mail; I always went to pick up my cheques in person, so people would remember me.

I went straight to the reception house where I'd recently played for my friends' wedding and had the light bulb conversation about candles with the owner. 'Matt, how are you my friend? Come, let's have a coffee.' That's exactly what I wanted; a happy greeting and a coffee would give me at least five minutes to pitch to him my proposal to become his (and everyone in his network's) candle supplier.

'You remember last week, after I performed at my friends' wedding, we sat in your office and over a coffee spoke briefly about candles and the lack of quality suppliers?' I then paused for a minute, as the owner was staring at me with a look of confusion; either he didn't remember or couldn't believe I'd picked up on the business opportunity he'd directly pitched to me. 'Well, I have solved that problem for you.'

I placed a standard industry candle with the exact requirements he'd described right in front of him, with a great big smile of confidence on my face. 'These actually have a burning time of seven hours, one more than you need. How great is that?' We sat in silence for a moment, which seemed like hours. 'Matt, leave it with me; have a great day.' He finished his coffee, grabbed the candle and walked off. This was the DJ demo scenario all over again. But this time I was a little more educated, I knew how to be patient.

The rest of that day I made my way to the other wedding venues, having coffees, collecting payments, but never mentioning the candle venture, as I wanted the first owner I met with to be the pioneer. He owned the biggest group of reception venues in the industry, so whatever he did, the rest followed.

I arrived home that evening and checked my emails; there was nothing from him. I was disappointed, but didn't really think too much about it. Something had to happen, I knew it, there were too many signs leading up to this. I'd found it so easy to construct a business plan for importing something from overseas that I literally had no idea about. I'd had to learn on the fly, which I did so quickly.

I had everything ready to go: the supplier, shipping company and transport delivery company. I even had a small warehouse lined up with a friend of mine.

I sat down to dinner with my parents that night. We were halfway in when my phone rang. I usually either let the phone ring out or put it on vibrate. That night I answered, and it was the reception owner, the one who'd taken my sample candle with no feedback. 'Matt, come in tomorrow and let's talk details about the candles. I burnt it today and you're right, it actually burnt for eight hours, there was no scent, and it was dripless, exactly what I need. Be here at nine o'clock in the morning and we can talk.'

I hung up the phone and just stared into space, with a palette of mixed emotions. When colours collide, you don't know what the final outcome will be but it looks as if the colours are having the greatest time being mixed in with one another, not knowing or caring what will be the final outcome; they are at peace in the present moment and in their element of creation.

'Who was that and what did they want?' my dad asked, wondering who would be so rude to disturb us at our family dinner. 'Oh, it was one of the reception owners. They may have some more work for me, so I need to go in the morning to see him.' I didn't want to go into details with my parents, not because I didn't think they'd understand—hell, I didn't know fully what I was doing—but I wanted to secure everything first, then show them the results.

That night I finished dinner, raced to my room and started to work on contracts and the finer details: how long manufacture would take, delivery, minimum orders and, of course, payment methods.

Now I knew in the back of my mind that I had to order a minimum of five pallets per month for six months, in order to get a very good rate from the supplier. So I had to ensure the buyers would be locked into a contract that would cover my minimum orders, and I had to be creative and not use any of my own funds, to minimise risk.

The next day I was up early and made my way to the reception house. I arrived an hour early but luckily the owner was there. To be honest, I'd only had about two hours' sleep the night before, but I had constructed a very strategic business plan. If all went well, this would be one of the greatest business moves I had made to date. We sat down and he didn't waste any time. 'I like your product; what are your terms and what's it going to cost me?' So I didn't waste time with my terms and presenting him with my proposal.

If you know how to get it, up-to-date information is the most valuable commodity in life. Luckily for me, I knew how to get it. I knew one of the girls who worked upstairs in the office at that particular venue and asked her on the quiet to see how much they were paying per individual candle. That way I could ensure I was supplying a superior product and at a lower cost as well.

In business you always need to hold the cards. In order for this candle venture to work, I needed to know what he was paying per unit. The product was important but I knew that price was the breaking point for these guys, If I could supply them the same candle with longer burning time for fifteen cents cheaper per unit, the deal would be made.

'Well, my terms are simple. I will provide you with the same candle you tested, for the displayed non-negotiable price per individual unit, but you must order a minimum of two pallets per month. We will implement an eight-month contract to ensure you receive this incredible low price each month and you pay fifty percent upfront and fifty percent on delivery. You will have your first shipment in four weeks.'

There it was, a pitch that saw him drooling at the mouth, as he knew he was saving money. He knew me as a person, so the trust factor as a supplier was already in play. I had basically erased any risk personally as I would use his deposit, more than I needed to purchase the shipment and pay for the transport to Sydney, and I would still make almost ninety percent profit.

'What if I ordered ten pallets from you per month, and got all of the other owners to order from you. Can you give me, and only me, a better price and deal?' In business you need to have the ability to think on your feet; every word that comes out of your mouth must be delivered with confidence and from education, both formal and self-taught. Your answers need to count and not be driven by emotion. Luckily that day, my words were probably the most strategic and educated they have ever been.

'If you can have all of the other reception venues in your network on board by close of business today, with their deposits paid by close of business tomorrow, that will allow me to place an order straightaway and have your candles to you in four weeks from tomorrow. I will not give you a cheaper rate but, as a token of my appreciation, I will provide you with one pallet of candles each month at no charge.'

Who was I kidding? If this guy was about to provide me with the opportunity to supply nearly every top end reception house in the game with candles, and my profit margin so high, I would gladly give him a free pallet. I could afford that offer as the profits were so high.

'Matt, I will call you at four thirty this afternoon with a verdict.' We shook hands and I made my way back home, trying to work out what had just happened and where my instant CEO negotiation skills had come from. If I were to pull off this deal … I hadn't yet worked out the figures, but I knew they were huge … it would be like pulling a rabbit out of a hat.

That was probably the longest day I'd ever had to sit through. I was like an expecting father, pacing, checking my phone and watching the time. It was four o'clock that afternoon, only half an hour to go. I thought I'd kill time by checking emails and replying to my unanswered inbox.

When I opened my inbox I saw more than fifty unread emails. Now this wasn't so unusual; I often had a lot of unread emails at the one time, with so many events happening each week. What made my heart jump out of its chest on this occasion was that every email subject read: *Candle Order Request.*

He had done it and kept to his word. I had all of the top reception houses requesting contracts to order their pallets of candles with the same terms and conditions as the main guy, except that he would receive a kickback of free pallets for his referrals.

I could not believe my eyes; then my phone rang. You know when you are deeply engulfed in something and then your phone rings and it's as loud as a car horn and right in your face. Well, that's what my phone sounded like. It was the reception house owner that I had met with that day.

'Matt, have you checked your inbox?' 'Yes I have; I am looking at it now,' I replied. 'So looks like you have a long night ahead of you, writing contracts and sending invoices. I look forward to receiving my candles in four weeks, along with my complimentary pallet.' 'I look forward to personally delivering them to you my friend, thank you,' I happily replied. We spoke for a little longer discussing minor details, and ended the conversation with the owner saying very clearly, 'Matt, don't let us down, because if you do, you will never work in this industry again!'

That didn't scare me, it actually drove me to ensure the business would work and move forward to make sure my clients, now almost sixty reception houses in Sydney, received a great product, service and price.

I went on to supply a total of 73 venues, a mixture of wedding reception venues, high end restaurants, luxury lodges and day spas. I was the middleman, ordering candles from overseas. The pallets would be secured every month as per each contract, paid for in advance, and the transport would be ready to go a day after the pallets arrived in Sydney, so I didn't even have to pay for a warehouse.

Combining the candle business and DJ'ing I was earning six figures a month, more than what some people earn in four years of working a full-time day job—all with no formal education, just a will to learn, and the ability to see signs as signs, not coincidences, when they were deposited in front of me.

Starting that candle business gave me some much-needed confidence. Unfortunately, I also became well into ego. I was earning ridiculous amounts of money each month, my DJ career saw me travelling the country weekly; and I was happy.

I even started a vending and separate sister advertising business, which saw me house over 200 machines Australia wide, with advertising sold on the front of each machine.

But no matter how much money I earned, and how busy and popular I became, I continued to stay on the path of fast food, late nights, energy drinks and minimal sleep, a lethal combination which I didn't think about at the time. But somehow in the back of my mind I knew this couldn't last for long. As much as I was enjoying it from the outside, my insides were being abused and this time I was the abuser.

Other people had abused me for years, and emotionally I felt the effects. I said to myself that I would never treat anyone as I had been treated. But what I never said was that I would never treat **myself** as others had treated me. Without realising it, that's what I was doing.

I was abusing myself internally with lack of sleep, fast fake food, being always on the go. I didn't have any structure, no happy place, no 'me' time and I couldn't see the damage it was doing. But it would be something that would be felt not just by me, but by everyone in my life who knew me, loved me, and who would grow to know me.

Chapter 10

The Art of Business

So how's things Matt? Haven't seen you in a while; Mum tells me you have been travelling a lot.

As my businesses grew and my DJ career skyrocketed, I was hardly home. I hardly saw my family, including my brother. My brother and I tried to catch up for a lunch every month, which more times than not would eventuate into a business meeting. But even that was sometimes impossible, as my schedule was out of control.

'Yes, I have been really busy; entertainment has been great and I've started a few other side businesses.' I could easily talk to my brother about business; he was a well-rounded businessman, so it was always good to bounce ideas off him. But I never went into how much I was earning or the extent of my work. For some reason, I felt that he wouldn't entirely understand how I could earn so much money with so little education. So I always watered things down.

He never gave off a negative vibe in any way; it was just one of those misconceptions we humans create. He loved the candle venture, thought it was genius, even asked to buy into it. I said it wasn't big enough for that yet; who was I kidding? It was, but I didn't want him to know that.

We had a great catch up that day, talking about business, family, life. We ate like kings, my brother picked up the bill as he always did, and we gave each other a hug. He left me with these final words, words that I would think about over time: 'Look forward to what's next for you, little brother.'

What's next? Wow I didn't even think about what was next for me, what I was doing was enough. Now my brother had just put another deposit into my thoughts, leaving me thinking even further about the art of business. I loved business; I loved the art of it, the chase and especially closing the deal.

I had created a number of successful businesses which were almost running themselves, so I thought to myself: *If I can do that with those, what else can I do it with?* I wanted more, I was driven and hungry for more, I was ready to start my mighty empire, build my own world, and nothing was going to bring me down.

I was driving home that day and halfway into my journey I felt a sharp pain in my stomach and an urge to go to the bathroom. I could hold it but not for long. I found the nearest shopping centre, and just made the toilet in time.

I sat on the toilet for quite some time in excruciating pain. I was sweating and had acute diarrhoea. I couldn't work out why. After about half an hour I felt there was nothing left; and when I wiped my burning bum there was blood on the toilet paper.

I didn't know what to do. I wiped again, more blood then, as I looked in the toilet bowl, I was dripping blood from my rectum like a leaking tap. I panicked but kept wiping, thinking the bleeding would stop. I didn't know what to do, so I waited. After about ten minutes, the bleeding stopped. I wiped until there was hardly any blood, packed my underwear with toilet paper in case I bled on the way home, and rushed out of the toilet block into my car.

On the way home, I can remember feeling very scared. This wasn't the first time I had bled; it had first happened over a year ago, but that wasn't as heavy as today. Everything my brother and I had spoken about that day was totally erased from my mind. At the forefront were two things: one was obvious—the bleeding; the second was that I had no idea what was happening to me so fear was painted throughout my body.

I arrived home and everyone was out. I went to the bathroom to assess how bad the situation was and whether the bleeding had stopped. It had, but my underwear and jeans were covered in blood.

It was horrible; I jumped straight into the shower and quickly washed myself before anyone arrived home. I wanted to dispose of my clothes, as though they were evidence from somebody I had just killed. I grabbed my pants and underwear, threw them in the bin and went for an afternoon sleep, as I was rather dizzy by that time.

I woke up just before dinner that day. To be honest, it felt as though a bus had hit me. I sat down at the dinner table, looking like death warmed up. 'See son, I told you that you are doing too much, you need to slow down.' 'Yeah dad you're right, I will, don't worry,' I replied, knowing it wasn't my busy work schedule that was making me tired, it was something deeper.

My father saw I was working hard; I was never home. He would constantly tell me to slow down. I would always brush him off, thinking he was just a concerned father. But maybe he was right, and maybe this was life telling me to slow down. Maybe it was time to listen.

That night, I completed some paperwork for my companies. While sitting in front of the computer I felt a sudden pain then, within a split second, a sharp stabbing in my stomach. Then it hit me without warning, the gates to my bowel were opening and I knew I needed to go to the toilet and it needed to be **now**!!

I ran to the bathroom and, by the time I had my pants down, it was already on its way out; but not what usually exits. This was blood again, this time heavier and, when I wiped, there was what I know today to be red, bloody mucus.

At that point, I can remember thinking one thing and that was: *I am dying*. Now I wasn't dying, but I felt close to it. The blood was rushing out of me and I couldn't stop it. I literally had to sit there and wait until it had ceased and hope my parents wouldn't come and ask why I had been in the toilet for so long. Luckily my family knew we all had sensitive stomachs, so we were all tolerant in that area. But this wasn't a sensitive stomach, this was something else.

I went to bed that night more exhausted than I had ever been; even after DJ'ing for more than twenty nights straight with only three hours sleep a night. It just didn't make sense. I was in a state of panic but not educated enough to know what was happening. So I did what most males in a place of ego would do. I went to bed hoping to wake up the next morning with the problem gone. If it hadn't, I would ignore it until it did, or live with it until it stopped me in my tracks.

For the next month, I found myself bleeding off and on. I would be fine for a day, then I would bleed for two; pain would hit like a freight train and the sense of urgency to go to the toilet was indescribable. If I didn't find a toilet within thirty seconds, it was all over for my pants. This situation would be the set-up for the beginning of a life-changing experience, which took the art of business right out from under my feet.

I was DJ'ing a guest spot, playing for two hours in a new hot spot nightclub in Sydney. By this time, what was happening to me physically was happening too often. So I'd kind of worked out a system and had emergency procedures of my own in place, to adapt to my unwanted symptoms. I wouldn't eat too much before a gig; I would have spare clothing in the boot of my car; I wore two pairs of underwear in case I bled during a DJ set; and I always wore dark clothing, so the blood wouldn't be seen. The only thing I couldn't forward think was when and where the urgency would hit; this was a matter of chance.

I placed my first record on the turntable; it was a massive track at the time and the crowd went crazy. Now usually when I DJ, I bounce around shaking my hands; the crowd was my drug and I would be high. But this night, I played the right songs but my energy levels were low. I wasn't moving, just playing a physiological game with myself, hoping I wouldn't need to rush to the toilet during my set.

In most cases it would be fine. If I had a meeting on during the day I would begin by saying that I'd had some bad food the night before and it was repeating on me, so please excuse me if I need to use the bathroom all of a sudden. Most of the time that would work. But in a DJ booth, it's just you and the music, each song a duration of about three minutes. So if you needed to go to the toilet, too bad. To make matters worse, the next DJ to play after you would usually show up a full five minutes before their set, so there was no saviour in them either.

I was doing okay until about an hour and ten minutes in. I was almost at the finish line, sweaty and shaking from the mental hunger game I was playing with myself, hoping I wouldn't need to go.

It was the peak of the night. I dropped the hottest track out at the time and I will never forget it—the crowd went crazy; more than a thousand hands were in the air. The MC standing on a podium in the middle of the dance floor was hyping the crowd even further. Then it hit me— instant pain in my stomach and urgency. I felt the sharpest pain and I needed to get to the bathroom; my deepest fear had become reality.

I looked around, trying to find a lifeline, anyone I knew to come and just stand behind the turntables while I ran to the bathroom. There was no-one. I scanned the room like a robot, trying to find an instant solution. My mind was racing through scenarios, as though it was a computer running through code, trying to identify a virus. Then it all came to a crashing halt.

I felt my bowel start to loosen and release, so I clenched my rectum, hoping it would hold off what was about to happen. It only made things worse and sped up the process.

I think back now and laugh, as I am sure there was someone watching me that night. Perhaps an up-and-coming wannabe DJ, as I'd once been, sitting in the corner and watching the person he wanted to be.

If such a person were in the club that night, they would have seen someone on stage controlling the crowd with his fingertips and, at the same time, sweating as though he had just dived into a pool and displaying the most profound expressions of pain, struggle and confusion.

That night I didn't make it to the bathroom; my pants housed a pile of faeces, blood, and mucus, enough to fill four baby nappies. I DJ'd the rest of my set not moving an inch, from fear it would all fall out. I didn't bleed through; my double underwear and dark jeans just covered it for me. That night had to be one of the most embarrassing and soul destroying nights of my life.

As soon as my set was finished, I walked slowly to the bathroom. Before I knew it I had broken down in tears. I cried that night in the nightclub toilet, sitting there with my pants down, blood still dripping out of me but thankfully into the toilet bowl, wondering how I was going to come out of this without anyone knowing and so salvage any dignity I had left.

After what seemed like two hours, but in real time was only twenty minutes, I collected my thoughts and began to construct a plan for cleaning the mess up and getting out of the club into my car.

Now as much as it had been hell working in the sign-writing business, there was one valuable lesson the boss had taught me: when packing the car for an on-site job, to visualise yourself already at the job, doing the job and finishing the job. This helped illustrate what was needed tools wise for all aspects of that job.

So that's what I did; I visualised how to clean myself and get out of the situation with minimal damage to my ego. First step was to get my underwear off slowly, without getting any blood on my pants, shoes or socks. So like a surgeon with steady hands, I slowly removed my pants with no leakage. Next step was the hardest, wiping my rear end.

As I reached for the toilet paper I found myself in my first predicament: there wasn't any left on the roll. This wasn't the night for me to be facing an empty toilet roll; what was I to do? If I couldn't wipe myself clean and dry, people in the club would notice as I walked out. Think, Matt, think!!

That night created habits that I still live with today. It was such a traumatic experience for me that, to this day, I still use forward thinking when planning most of my activities. Today, when using a public toilet, the first thing I do is check whether there is a full roll of paper. I always lift the seat up when I'm finished (as most males urinate on them), then if someone like me rushes in needing to go, they don't waste time wiping the seat. And nine times out of ten, no matter how hot it is, I wear a singlet ... why, you ask?

That night I had been in a predicament. I needed to clean myself and there was nothing to clean myself with. I needed a plan. I literally stopped, prayed and asked the higher source to guide me out of this situation. I begged, pleaded and when I took my hands out of the praying position, my chain got caught on the singlet I was wearing under my shirt.

This was an indirect light bulb moment, like I'd had with the candles, except this one was life saving, not business creating. I thought to take my shirt off, then my singlet and rip it up using my keys as a knife. My singlet was thicker than toilet paper so, in theory, this had to work. I started to cut and rip, cut and rip, until I had a pile of rags ready to absorb the blood.

I wiped the areas that were bloody, using my mobile phone to take photos and see where I was bleeding, so I didn't waste any singlet rag. It worked; I was clean—well clean as I could be—but here was my next problem. I couldn't flush the singlet, as it would have clogged up the toilet. I had no idea what I was going to do.

Allow me to mentally paint a word picture for you … I was sitting in a nightclub toilet with my shoes to my right, my jeans hanging on the hook behind the door, my socks in my shoes, my shirt sitting on my shoes as they were the cleanest items of clothing I had; to my left were two piles, one with two bloody pairs of underwear and the other with a torn up singlet soaked in blood.

At that point I didn't see any exit strategy at all. I still had to work out a way to stop the bleeding, throw the evidence away in the bathroom bin, head back to the DJ booth, grab my records, make my way back to the car and then drive home.

The car was my safe house. I didn't care what happened from that point on, as no-one was there. It would be too late in the morning when I arrived home for my parents to see the state I was in.

I took my time working out a scenario and the best thing I could do was wait. I needed either someone half sober in the next toilet to get me some toilet paper, or I was stuck in that toilet until close.

About fifteen minutes later, I heard the toilet door next to me close. In a nightclub, you can usually sense those who are drunk or on drugs.

They talk to themselves and laugh a lot, or are totally the opposite and want to fight with everyone.

When the guy sat down next to me it was as though my superhero senses were switched on. I watched his shadow and he took his time to wipe the toilet seat—no drunken person would do that—and he was on the phone, arguing with his girl friend. This was perfect, he had to be nice to me.

I wasted no time yelling out: 'Excuse me, thank God you came. I am the guy to your left and have no toilet paper. Could you please pass over a bundle?' As easy as that! I heard the toilet roll spin fast, as though he wanted to get rid of me and continue arguing with his girlfriend, and there it was, a bunch of toilet paper sitting on the floor between his and my toilet cubicles.

I can not express the joy that radiated from my soul at that point. I had an exit strategy but I needed to keep a clear head. I used half the toilet paper to wrap up my underwear and bloody singlet, so I could throw it in the bin after leaving the toilet cubicle. Then I used my two socks to plug my anus up and the remainder of the toilet paper to wrap around my lower body, holding the socks in place to absorb the blood still leaking from me.

After pulling up my jeans, I ever so gently opened the toilet door, to see if anyone was around. There was no-one; this was my chance. I raced out, threw the bundle in the rubbish and washed my bloody hands.

Now all I had to do was make it to the stage, grab my stuff and get out but I didn't anticipate how hard that was going to be. I was quite popular in the DJ world at that time and knew just about everyone at the club. So there were lines of people wanting to talk, high fiving me, grabbing me in every direction possible, which only made my anxiety levels soar from worrying that my pants would burst open, spraying blood all over the crowd like a scary horror movie. I did my best to move through the crowd, engaging in minimal conversation, enough to avoid appearing rude or as if something was wrong.

I eventually made it to the stage and, thankfully, the DJ that was on had packed my record box and needles up for me, as he needed the room. He didn't realise how big a favour he did for me that night. I grabbed my cases, didn't even say goodbye and walked out, trying not to eyeball and catch anyone's attention.

I drove home so slowly that night with the music off and window down, crying my eyes out and feeling so alone.

I arrived home at four in the morning, ran straight to my room and unwrapped myself. I had stopped bleeding. I placed the toilet paper and socks in two plastic bags, put them under my bed so my parents wouldn't find them, and sank into bed.

I didn't sleep much that night. I tried but was so anxious and afraid, my body shook and my tears flowed like a river all night. Eventually I fell asleep and slept most of that Sunday, my usual procedure so my parents didn't think much of it. They came in every now and then, to confirm that I was breathing. My mother opened my window to let in fresh air and left a sandwich next to my bed.

I ate nothing that Sunday and got out of bed eight times to go to the bathroom. Every time there was blood. I was feeling exhausted and knew this wasn't going away and I needed to see a professional ASAP.

But I couldn't. I had a massive shipment of candles coming in that week that I needed to oversee; I had to be there. Whatever was happening healthwise, I needed to forget. I had business to take care of.

That was the problem; I always put everything else before me: family, friends and business, never allowing myself 'me' time. We spend our whole lives chasing the dollar and, when we catch it, we then spend all of our wealth on medical bills trying to regain what we have lost through the wealth-chasing, health-neglecting years.

That week was huge for me. I had twelve containers of candles coming in, which amounted to huge profit gains. I had some of the biggest events to organise and was also doing two guests spots in two different states.

I don't know how I successfully pulled everything off. My candles landed in the country and I organised the couriers to deliver them to their destinations; my entertainment company provided a full roster of DJs; and I played at the two interstate gigs. But each day saw me bleeding more and more, not eating, having extreme urgency, losing weight, and my eyes became dark, with bags like an old man. I even started to lose the hair on my head. And did I mention I had high interest in someone wanting to buy my vending and advertising business?

The Monday after that big week I woke up at nine in the morning. My window was open so I knew my mother was awake. The room was spinning; I was lacking energy but feeling hungry. I tried to call out to my mother but my bedroom door was closed and, to be honest, my yell was only a whisper due to my lack of energy.

So I struggled and made my way out of bed, put my slippers on and walked slowly to my door. My mum was having breakfast and happily greeted me but the expression on her face changed as she saw the state I was in. She asked what was wrong and all I can remember was seeing two of her; the room went blurry and everything went black.

I woke up in a hospital bed in emergency, with five doctors standing around me, an oxygen mask strapped to my face, drips out of three parts of my body and my father cradling my weeping mother.

Chapter 11

Colour Me Lucky

We need to get the blood tested, and check the results ASAP!

The doctors had momentarily left my hospital bed. I can remember them looking at me without saying a word, quite perplexed. They needed to go away and come up with a game plan; I heard one say that my blood results would determine the diagnosis.

My mother had gone to get a coffee so it was just my father and me. He was crying, but kept it together as best he could. At first he didn't say too much; I remember trying to work out the expression on his face. I think it was a combination of sadness, confusion, worry and a little disappointment.

I knew straight away that he would blame my DJ career and lifestyle; he had never been a big fan of that part of my life. He spoke to me softly, trying to work out how I came to be lying in the emergency room on what seemed to be my deathbed. 'Son are you okay? What happened?' That's all that came out of my father's mouth. I couldn't answer; I had no energy. All I can remember doing was grabbing his hand and winking at him, as tears ran down both of our faces. Words weren't needed, just being together was enough at that time.

A few moments later I heard yelling; it was my brother demanding to see me. My father raced over to bring him to me—great timing, as my family are all a little hot-blooded, especially my brother. When it comes to family, we fight for each other.

As he approached my bed, I could see him tear up. My brother didn't know what had happened; all he had been told was that I been admitted to hospital in an ambulance. That information had been explained by a nurse, as my parents had been too distraught to talk to him.

My brother stood on one side of the bed and my father the other; it was as though they knew something I didn't. They both stood there holding my hands. I drifted in and out of consciousness until my father couldn't handle it anymore and walked off crying, trying to find my mother so they could comfort each other.

I woke up the next morning in a room with three other men, all around eighty years of age. And here I was … I should have been a fit, healthy, happy young man but here I was the total opposite, a picture of near death.

I woke to see my mother and father sitting by the window. My mother noticed me wake up and slapped my father quickly, to go and alert the doctors. 'Hello son, you scared us for a minute you know.' My mother was holding my face crying, but I think it was a mixture of painful and joyful tears, as my eyes were open at last.

Before I knew it, my father was back. Behind him followed what I still think of as an army of doctors with clipboards ready to takes notes, looking important but rarely coming up with a clear answer for anyone. Usually there is one doctor in charge, who delegates. Depending on their personality, that doctor confronts you with facts that often have no relevancy to your condition, not caring about your state of mind and treating you as though you are lower than dirt.

Thankfully, on this occasion I had a caring doctor. He sat next to me on my bed and I remember him saying, 'You are quite the lucky boy. I would colour you lucky if I could, right now.'

Now a male's blood count and haemoglobin levels should be *around* 120 on average, over 100 is good. After multiple tubes of blood were extracted from my body and the results came back, my blood count was at 45 (intensive care is around 41). However, I was still functioning, not great but still functioning, and this doctor couldn't believe how or why.

He went on to ask a question that I didn't want my parents to hear, as I knew they would get angry, but there was nowhere to hide: 'How long have you been losing blood?' With the little energy I had I whispered, 'A few weeks now.' As soon as I said that, I saw my parents look at each other, their eyeballs popping out of their heads, wondering how they could have missed that and why I hadn't told them. They didn't say anything, they kept quiet, and we all listened to the doctor and his team of clipboards. My brother was in the room which was good, because he asked the right questions when needed.

The result was they needed to pump multiple bags of blood into my body to replace the blood loss and also inject me with daily bags of iron. When you lose blood you lose iron, which explained why I had been so tired. They also needed to conduct a colonoscopy, to go inside and see why I was bleeding.

This explanation took about half an hour. The doctor touched my forehead as though he had known me for years and said, 'Don't worry, we will fix you.' He smiled and walked off.

For the next four days, I would be pumped with bags of blood, followed by bags of iron. But when it came to the iron infusions, I had a bad reaction with the first bag, so the doctor ordered a watered-down lighter version, as my body was sensitive to the normal one.

Finally, colour started to return to my face. I wasn't allowed to eat, so I was on a drip. I was pretty hungry but found myself not going to the toilet as much, so I didn't care for food.

By the sixth morning, I was sitting up in bed; I was communicating and even cracking jokes here and there. It was time for the posse of doctors with their clipboards to make their presence felt; but that day didn't go as usual.

That day my specialist, the caring doctor, came alone. He walked in, said good morning to us all, then pulled the curtains around my bed so no-one could see us; that was never a good sign. He asked how I was feeling, mentioned I looked much better, I knew he was conducting small talk. My heart was racing; I really had no idea what he was about to say, but had a feeling it wasn't going to be positive.

'The results from your colonoscopy are back. Combined with your blood tests, we can now confirm what and where the bleeding is from. You have developed a disease called Ulcerative Colitis, which is an inflammatory bowel disease. We don't know how you developed it, there is no cure, and it can only be managed by medication.'

An ulcerative what? I had never heard of such a thing; my parents and I just looked at each other. Coming from a relatively healthy family, this was a bullet to the heart.

'Doctor, what does this mean?' Surprisingly, my mother broke the silence. 'Well, his bleeding has stopped thankfully. So we want to keep him here for a few more days to monitor him. Then we will start him on a medication process that he will need to maintain for quite some time.'

I kept quiet; I was a pretty positive person but the demons of panic were screaming inside me. You see, when someone calls you a name or disrespects you verbally, you can just dismiss it—they are only words so they can't hurt you, they don't physically exist. But when someone, especially a doctor, labels you with a disease for the rest of your life, it takes your emotions to a whole new level.

I instantly thought I was going to die, or live as a disabled person. Negative dark emotions started to sweep through my mind, resulting in me involuntarily throwing up on my hospital bed. And the worst thing was that I couldn't go anywhere or move out of the way, as I had several drips in my body attached to various monitors. So my mother had to call a nurse while I sat in my own vomit.

As I sat there crying, staring at my vomit, my father stroked my head and told me everything was going to be fine. I didn't care what he had to say at that time; I was angry that life had dealt me this blow.

I had always been nice to people, even after all of the abuse I had copped in my earlier working years. I'd worked hard; I was a business owner making a substantial and honest living. Why was I now being punished with this disease; and not just any disease but an incurable one. I was furious!

I told my father to leave me alone; I wanted to be by myself. He hesitated but eventually went into the hospital corridor and my mother followed. I sat on the chair staring at the nurses cleaning my bed, still attached to the machine that was feeding multiple drips into my arm.

I wanted to rip the drips out, take off that stupid hospital robe and get back to the life I'd had before this crap. But who was I kidding? I had no energy, could hardly walk from being in bed for so many days straight and had poor blood circulation. But all I could see and feel was anger.

Looking back now, my emotional state was playing a powerful tune. And when emotion takes over intelligence, humans have no hope; ego creeps in and everything that you once saw in a strategic and calm way flies right out the door.

But what I didn't realise back then was that I was about to enter a process. A process of learning, change, personal development, spirituality and self-discovery, taught by the highest teacher the world has to offer: life itself.

I often say today that I was blessed and am thankful that I was diagnosed with a medical condition. Most times people look at me with confusion on their faces. I explain that the reason I am thankful is because I went into hospital with one set of eyes and came out looking through a whole new set. I learnt things throughout my education (meaning my illness years) that most people never get to tap into in this life. Now I am able to see the physical world in a whole new light.

But that's wisdom speaking and that is only learnt through pain. When I was diagnosed that day I was in pain, physically and mentally. I was confused, angry, tired, dizzy and wallowing in fear. These are all dangerous emotions that did not help my condition at all. Every time I felt some sort of discomfort, it would directly hit my stomach; then instantly the sense of urgency would arise and I would need to use the bathroom toilet there and then. If I didn't, my pants would become the bathroom once again.

Later that day my brother came to visit me. I pretended to be asleep; I'd had enough crying that day. I heard my parents telling him what the doctors had said. He didn't say much but I could feel his presence very strongly that day. I could feel his sadness as I tried my hardest to fake sleep. My stomach was churning and I wanted to burst into tears but I held it together.

I pretended to be asleep until visiting hours were over that night. It was nine o'clock, everyone had left, it was just me lying in my bed with the three elderly men in theirs.

I remember looking outside the window and thinking: *I shouldn't be here, this isn't right.* I looked over to the elderly men and then back to me and couldn't work out what was going on. The nights were quiet in the hospital; you would hear the beeps of machines, footsteps of nurses and the occasional scream of patients. For the weeks I was there, it felt like a prison.

I didn't sleep a wink that night; I think I cried most of it. I spoke to God a lot that night, begging him to tell me why he had put me there. That was my ego talking, as I know now that God only puts the strongest soldiers through pain, those that come out of it ready for greatness.

Now I don't think I am 'of greatness', but know I am here to serve the greatness of God. How do I know that? During my illness, I should have left this earth many times but I always came back, due to continued teachings by the higher source each time I was struck by physical pain.

I remained in the hospital for thirteen days total. Each day consisted of blood transfusions, daily tests to assess my blood count, stool monitoring to monitor the blood in each movement and whether it had stopped, and strong doses of three different types of medication.

Added to that, I had daily visits from family and friends. At the time, I really didn't want to see anyone, as I was rushing to the toilet every five minutes. I needed help with that, due to the monitors attached to me; if they weren't disconnected quickly enough, I would release in my bed. Luckily my father worked out a system. He would always sit next to the power points and be ready to disconnect, pull the bed sheet off me and carry me to the closest toilet, when I gave him the signal.

'Well Matt, your blood count is constant, which means your blood loss has stopped. This is great, you are eating now, so I think the best thing is we let you go home; you continue with the medication process that I prescribe for you and we'll have regular check–ups. How does that sound?'

For the first time in thirteen days I smiled. It felt as though I were being released from prison. I started to cry which confused the doctor, but I told him they were tears of joy. He organised my release papers and I put on my civilian clothes, with the little energy I had. My mother helped with my shoes, as my father went to get the car.

Leaving the hospital that day was a bittersweet moment. I walked out with my mother holding me, as I literally had no energy and my leg muscles were almost non-existent. I was happy to be leaving, but unsure and scared of the road ahead, trying not to think too far ahead of my next move. I made my way to the front of the hospital where my father was waiting, slowly entered the car, closed my eyes and just enjoyed the journey home.

When I returned home that day, the house felt as though it was new; nothing had changed, it just felt new. All I wanted to do was soak in a bath. So as per my request and ever so gently, my parents ran the warm water for the bath, and started to help me get undressed. That's when I screamed out, 'No, let me do it! I won't lock the door, just let me do it!!.' They reluctantly let me be, closed the door halfway just in case something happened and, with the little energy I had, I made my way into a bath full of cleansing salts as though I were cleansing my soul.

I probably stayed in that bath for an hour that day; I needed my father to help me get out, I couldn't lift a finger. He helped me dry off and get dressed; then walked me to a chair in the lounge room and went to make me something to eat.

I can remember sitting down and feeling a little light-headed. While my mother was in my room putting fresh sheets on my bed, my father was making me some lunch. I can remember gazing over to the lounge room window where my eyes squinted from the brightness of the sun. All I wanted to do was embrace it, so I used all of my strength to push up from the armrest and made my way to the front door. I think a snail could have beaten me, at the pace I was going. I finally reached the front door, luckily it was unlocked, and I slowly walked down the front steps to the driveway.

It probably took me about fifteen minutes to get from my lounge room chair to the driveway, which normally would take no more that a minute. I finally reached the spot on the driveway where the sun was shining, wearing black tracksuit pants, slippers, singlet and a flannelette shirt. I raised my head to the sun then I found my arms reaching out, as though I was about to fly. I felt that sun pierce my body and I had never felt such peace in my life.

I think back to that day at my parent's house. It was situated on a main road, so if anyone drove past that day in my moment of embrace, I can't imagine what they were thinking. But that wasn't in my thoughts at the time; I just embraced nature in its glory. Then my father came running outside, screaming at me, worried about how I'd got there and what in the world I was doing.

I remember opening my eyes and looking at him saying, 'I am just enjoying life Dad.' For a moment the world stopped; my father and I stood on our driveway, him holding me up, as my energy levels had started to lower and my body had started to shake. We both just embraced nature's beauty and appreciated something that money can't buy but that is there every day for each of us to enjoy.

I made my way back inside, ate my lunch and fell straight to sleep. I had no idea what was ahead of me. I didn't realise the journey I was about to embark on, no-one did. We all thought okay, I had been diagnosed with something, I'd take a few tablets to make everything better and that would be that. I'd go for regular check-ups and continue on with life.

That was our uneducated minds speaking to us, when I was released from hospital for the first time. I was about to enter a war zone, a war zone that consisted of inner demons, doctors, and everyday chores that would become challenges, sending my anxiety levels through the roof.

All of these elements almost killed me. I was tested in so many ways that I thought at times that there was no way I would make it through that particular situation or night.

My prayers and faith would be tested like nothing I ever thought existed. I would see things not of this world, and most times could not talk about, due to the intensity of each situation. I would battle so-called specialists that I foolishly handed my trust and life over to and, worst of all, I would battle my family, friends and myself.

I had been out of hospital for less than two months. I had built my weight back up, I had colour in my face, and I was just able to drive short distances. I had to have my blood count checked every week, to monitor a number of things including blood levels and sugar levels. Due to the amount of medication I was taking, I ran the risk of getting diabetes.

It was very tough having needles shoved in my arm every week. I was still quite weak from hospital but, to be honest, I was being viewed differently. I was a patient, a diagnosed diseased person. Every time I walked into a doctor or specialist appointment, I felt that energy start to impact on me emotionally.

When you're first diagnosed with a disease (well, I found it to be this way), your disease dictates your life. It becomes alive and lives through you; you become a passenger to your disease.

I would be sitting in rooms with elderly men thinking, *I shouldn't be here.* I still had stomach pain from my ulcers but I wasn't bleeding, which I was happy about, but I had a new friend—well, an enemy in real terms—and that was anxiety.

I had been a frequent user of the bathroom ever since I can remember; I really didn't think anything of it. But once you're diagnosed with Ulcerative Colitis, one of the symptoms that is confirmed to you is increased bowel movement. Really, what that meant was rapid bowel movement, without any control whatsoever. For some reason, since starting on the medication I had to go even more frequently. So the medication had stopped one problem, the bleeding, but increased another, the frequency of going to the toilet.

I would find myself literally going to the toilet fifteen times a day and this was on an empty stomach. I found it so hard to drive anywhere. As soon as I left my comfort zone, meaning home, I had to map out where the toilets were and be ready to jump out of the car. Most times I didn't make it.

As a male who'd been quite healthy prior to this and a self-employed businessman earning quite a healthy living, there was nothing more degrading to ones' self-esteem than losing bowel control while driving to a meeting.

This mode of living was not healthy for me, especially as I had Colitis. The best environment for a Colitis sufferer is one that is stress free and happy. But my life now felt like it was when I was an apprentice. I was living in fear; fear that when I went out, I would not make it to the bathroom. This created intense anxiety because, if I did lose control, I would have to strategically think how I could get to a bathroom without anyone seeing a big brown patch on my pants, before going on to whatever appointment I had and acting as though everything was happy times.

I found myself maintaining a minimal diet. I thought that if I didn't eat, I wouldn't need to go to a bathroom. Well that didn't work—even if I ate nothing for days, I would build up the anxiety of it possibly happening to me in the car, so as soon as I thought about it, my stomach would cramp up and release.

I kept my anxiety and car incidents to myself; my family knew I was going through a hard time, so they always knew if I came home and wasn't in a good mood to just leave me be.

My businesses started to lose traction. I found out that the person I'd hired to manage for me was stealing money from the business and not taking orders. I discovered this a week after returning home from hospital, when I opened my email account to find almost two hundred emails, all most abusive, from close clients I had built up over the years. I tried to mend those bridges and explain what had happened but, to be honest, they didn't care. It was their business and I was the face of mine. As the old saying goes: *There are no friends in business.* I found that was true very quickly.

So not only was I dealing with a newly-diagnosed disease, I now had to clean up the mess of my businesses and deal with the fact that I was almost bankrupt financially, and not from my own doing.

It was as though I had fallen into the body of someone else and was living a nightmare. But I wasn't; I was living my life and the shift had happened so quickly, I had blinked and missed it. Only now I had to wake up and deal with it.

The funny thing was, if I'd ever had a problem in my businesses I would always come up with a solution and fast. But facing the fact of having a disease, I couldn't; I didn't want to, I didn't know how to. So I did the only thing that a desperate person would do—I tried to take my own life.

That was on the day I found out I had been stolen from, and that my businesses were basically lost. I had just been to a check–up; I remember that I had to go to the toilet eight times on the way and the last time I stopped, there was a trickle of blood.

During my check–up, I didn't tell my doctor about it; I couldn't handle any more tests. My arms were black and blue from needles taking blood each day, not to mention the finger tests in my anus which made me feel violated. When I heard the doctor put his plastic glove on to do the test, I used to think: *Why am I letting him do this; surely there has to be an easier way?*

Why is it that when someone has the letters 'DR' in front of their name on their business card, we allow that person to control our lives and we do almost everything they say? Yet if our car breaks down and a mechanic gives us a diagnosis, nine times out of ten we will go to a couple of other mechanics to see if they give the same diagnosis. We don't hesitate to question their professional opinions.

I was at home that day after reading the emails and having my personal space invaded, and I was overwhelmed with anxiety. I was sitting at the computer staring at the screen, just wanting to scream. Not just scream, I wanted to roar! No-one was home so I could easily have done it, but I didn't. Instead I broke down in tears, the most heartfelt cry by myself to that date, and it didn't feel like it was going to stop.

Those tears turned to anger. I can remember cradling my face, then suddenly clenching my teeth. I could feel my temperature rising. I jumped up, threw my chair to the ground and walked to the kitchen, straight up to the medicine cabinet which housed my four containers of medication, two of which were very strong.

I grabbed the two strongest pills, opened my hands and poured them in, until all I saw was white. My theory was that if I took enough they would either kill me, stop the bleeding or the unknown.

In a world of mental pain, clear thinking isn't present! I filled my glass with water and started taking pill after pill, crying and screaming after each one. I knew what I was doing was wrong, but a little evil voice inside me was telling me to keep going, cheering me after each pill went down my throat.

I couldn't tell you how many pills I took that day. All I can say is I used to take three daily, and the doctors advised against taking more than prescribed, as the side effects could be lethal.

After devouring the tablets, I continued to cry and became angrier, walking around the house. But this wasn't any walk—I was powerwalking, pulling my hair, screaming, punching pillows. In the back of my mind, I prayed my parents didn't come home; I didn't want them to feel the wrath of whatever was happening.

I tired myself out and ended up in my room. I don't remember how I ended up there, but I fell into the deepest sleep I'd had in months. To be honest, I didn't expect to wake up that day and there was a part of me that didn't want to.

Apparently I slept for sixteen straight hours that day. I woke up with a lamp on next to me. I was undressed, just in boxer shorts, my window was open and a bottle of water was next to me, so I knew my parents were checking up on me. Thank God they didn't know what I had taken.

Physically, I felt the worst I had ever felt: raging headache, dizziness, pain in my stomach more present than ever, uncontrollable shakes, with anxiety and depression playing tennis in my mind.

I went to sit up in bed but fell straight back down. I needed a shower but I couldn't; there was no way I could stand up. Both of my parents tried to come into my room, to talk to me and help me out of bed. I was rude to them and told them to leave me alone; I was tired and would get up when I was ready.

Throughout my illness and to this day, there has always been one thing that I feel particularly sad about. Not the fact that I was sick nor the fact that I was almost bankrupt. It is the fact that taking the medication turned me into a different person. It made me an angry, bitter person. Unfortunately, as I lived under the same roof as my parents who loved and adored me, they always felt the evil end of my emotions.

I always knew that what I was doing or saying was wrong. It was always verbal; I would scream at them, call them names, tell them off for no apparent reason, then suddenly cry, as though the real me was floating back and noticing what I had said. Then I would break down with remorse.

To this day I still apologise to my parents. They say that no matter what I threw at them verbally they weren't going anywhere, as no-one could imagine what demons I was fighting.

I was fighting invisible demons that would attack me in my dreams, and in my thoughts when I was awake. I was a walking ghost, with no emotion and thinking the most polluted of thoughts.

Chapter 12

Don't Cry Over Spilt Paint

Son, what's wrong; apart from the obvious?

After my tablet incident, I ended up being bedridden for a week, except for rushing to the bathroom multiple times a day. Heavy blood loss continued, which I couldn't understand. It continued to infuriate and frustrate me as to why the stupid tablets weren't working; they had been prescribed to stop the bleeding and the urgency of going to the bathroom.

At this stage, I was crying uncontrollably every day, breaking down without warning and continuously shivering. My father sat next to my bed. I explained how I had lost a great deal of money in my business, how I couldn't control my bowel movements and how the tablets were making me angry. My depression and anxiety were at an all-time high and, to add salt to the wound, I admitted to my father that I had stopped going to the specialist. What was the point in going, when what they were prescribing wasn't helping me?

I didn't tell him about the near suicide attempt, he was worried enough. He went on to say something quite deep for my father at the time: 'Son, there's no point crying over spilt paint; those things happened in the past. We have to get you better and worry about the now, that's all son.'

I knew the message he was trying to get across without directly saying so: that it didn't matter about the money, he didn't care about the specialist and doctors, and all he wanted was his son to be his son again. And that's all I wanted too.

With my father's help, I got out of bed that day and had my first shower in weeks. At that point I was showering with my swimmers on, as my parents needed to sit outside the bathroom door, in case I collapsed from lack of blood.

That day was an eye-opener for my parents and me. I found myself starting to panic in the shower, the heat was getting to me and I started to panic like never before. My vision started to blur and the worst part was I looked down to see blood dripping from my anus. As soon as my brain registered what was happening, I started to panic even more; my heart started to beat faster, thumping as though it was about to burst out of my chest. I had no control over it.

I found out later that the reason why I had such high anxiety doing such a simple thing as having a shower was because I had lost so much blood. My heart literally had no blood to circulate to my other organs, to allow them to function normally. So they had to work overtime with the little blood I still had left.

The only way I can describe my increased heart rate experience in day-to-day terms is to think of the furthest you have ever jogged or the hardest form of exercise you have ever done. Double that, do that activity once, then do it again straightaway, all while being gagged at the mouth and under water with a shark chasing you—that's how bad it felt.

I screamed for help to get out of the shower that day and my father came rushing in, to find me on the floor shaking uncontrollably. He immediately turned the water off and yelled for my mother to call an ambulance. But I firmly refused. I didn't want to go back to hospital. I said I was okay, clearly I wasn't, and they both dried me ever so slowly and gently, dressing me in winter pyjamas. I was carried into the lounge room by my father and placed in front of the portable heater, with a blanket around me, to settle my shivering body and bring colour back to my lips.

About half an hour later my parents came and sat on the couch next to me. It was as though they had to go away and settle each other after what had happened. They were both crying as they looked at me and asked, 'Matt, are you bleeding again?' I didn't answer. 'Matt please tell us, have you been bleeding?' I didn't say anything, just nodded. 'For how long?' my father then asked. 'Why?' I replied angrily. Every time I was asked questions by my parents and especially by my doctors, I felt as though I was being interrogated. But I wasn't, it was my inner demons polluting my thoughts.

My mother got up and brought in the washing basket, containing the sheets I had been lying in for the previous week. They were drenched in blood. The blood loss must have been the result of the cocktail of medication I had taken a week earlier. I had been bleeding non-stop for a week and sleeping in it. No wonder I was so tired and felt as though a bus had run over me, picked me up thrown me against a wall, then run over me again.

My parents wanted to call an ambulance, they had the phone in their hand, but I insisted, 'I'm fine, just leave it a few more days, then we can reassess the situation. If I am the same then, you can call an ambulance.' Deep down I knew I wasn't going to last another week; I was going back to hospital, a place I hated, and there was no escaping it.

Against their will, my parents agreed to my request and, for the next two days, they monitored me around the clock. I was a walking zombie; I couldn't do anything for myself. Every time I tried to walk, the world would spin and I would need to hold onto something.

About three days later, my parents needed to go to the shops to buy groceries. They didn't want to leave me but my mother doesn't drive, so they had to go together. It would be a quick trip to buy the necessities.

It was around ten in the morning and I was barely awake. My father came in and asked if it was okay to leave me for an hour. In my polluted and angry state I replied, 'What a stupid question! Yes go, I don't care.'

I heard them lock the house and leave. I had not driven anywhere in weeks. It was a hot day; my car was parked outside in the driveway. Something inside told me to get up and move my car into the carport where my father's car normally parked, just in case I wanted to go out later that day. Then my car wouldn't be too hot to get into, as I had no air conditioning.

Now any normal person looking in on this situation would have recognised how unrealistic my thoughts were. Who was I kidding? I wasn't going anywhere anytime soon but I was sure I was, and I needed to move that car.

So with the little energy I had, I started to make my way out of my bed. I slowly put my dressing-gown on, no energy to put it on properly, just enough to wear it like a jacket. I walked ever so slowly to the front door, leaning on the walls and stopping constantly to catch my breath. I made it to the front door, my keys were right there, it took all my strength to unlock both security doors, but I did it.

Sluggishly, I walked in my slippers outside towards the driver's side of my car. I got inside, turned on the ignition and caught my breath, while the car warmed up. After ten minutes or so, I worked up enough confidence to put the car in reverse, ready to drive it into the carport. It took about seven attempts to line the car up straight in the carport, but I did it.

I was sitting in my car, already hot from the morning sun, sweating in my dressing–gown and boxer shorts, heart racing faster than ever. My small amount of energy had been used up by the little adventure I'd just had. My body was working overtime and once again I started to panic. I couldn't work out how I was going to make it safely back to bed without my parents' help.

After about twenty minutes, I talked myself into getting out of the car. I stepped out and took a step towards the front door. All I remember is seeing black, as the floor came closer to my face and that was it.

I woke up thirty minutes later, half of my body inside the house and the rest hanging out the front door. I looked down and saw blood all over my chest. My parents were not yet back from shopping.

There was no way I wanted them to see me like this, so I dragged myself along the floor, slamming the front door shut with my feet. I army crawled to the bathroom to find a face cloth, then wiped my chest and face to get rid of the blood, crawled back to my room, somehow got into bed and went to sleep.

Through all of this, I didn't even think about the time I'd spent lying outside the front door. My parents' home is situated on a main road, so people must have walked by and seen me. Did they look, see a body and just keep walking out of fear, or did they simply ignore me?

I also had forgotten that my car was parked in my father's spot; he would wonder why and how it got there when they arrived home. I'm not sure how long after they arrived home I woke up, got up for my usual toilet run, and my father quickly got up from his chair to ask how I was. 'Matt, what is your car doing in the carport?' he asked. 'I didn't want it to get hot.' My answer made no sense to him. I knew what I was talking about, I just didn't have the energy to explain and I didn't want to go into what had happened. Luckily he wasn't in a questionable mood that day and he dropped the subject.

I actually sat down at the dinner table that night, for the first time in almost three months. I didn't eat much, some boiled rice and half an egg—usually by that point I had started bringing it up. As I was sitting at the dinner table, I felt the sharpest of pains in the right side of my stomach. This pain was unlike the ulcers; they were a burning type of pain. This was a strong punch in the guts hard to breathe type of pain. I expressed my discomfort to my parents and was helped back to bed.

That night the pain kept increasing, no matter what I did or how many positions I tried to sleep in. This pain pounded away internally and I struggled to breathe. My frustration increased, which led to more pain, to the point where I couldn't lie straight in bed, I had to lie in the foetal position which gave a little relief.

For some reason, this was the only night my parents didn't check on me. Perhaps there was something happening higher in the universe that I wasn't aware of; something was brewing and I started to feel it. At that time, my illness was at its worst, and I couldn't see any light at the end of the tunnel.

I remember checking the time, it was two in the morning. I had been awake all night in a distressed state of mind. I had to make a decision, or perhaps it was already made for me? I knew what I had to do, without knowing what I was doing. I got out of bed, hunched over in agony and started to walk towards my door. While still in unbearable pain, I felt a weird sense of peace.

I made my way to the bathroom, opened the cabinet, grabbed a razor blade and shaving cream, turned on the shower, got undressed and made my way into the shower, all bent over from the pain in the right hand side of my body.

My father is a heavy sleeper but, at that time, a moth's fart would have woken him. As soon as he heard the shower, he raced downstairs in a state of panic.

'Matt, what the hell are you doing?' My father found me in the shower, naked and bent over, shaving cream all over my arms and legs and shaving myself. 'Matt, what the hell are you doing?' he yelled this time. I looked up at him and said weakly, 'Dad, please help me shave my body; I am going to hospital tonight and this time I want to go prepared. I don't want my arms and legs to be hairy, because when they tape the drip to my body the tape hurts as it grabs my hairs. Please help me Dad and when we are finished, call an ambulance.'

My father just stood there for a minute, as if he couldn't believe what he had just heard. I continued to shave my arms and he reluctantly went to the cupboard, retrieved a blade, and started to help me.

I can't imagine what was going through his mind at that time. It would have been very confronting to see your son, early in the morning, huddled over like an old man, shaving his body despite excruciating pain, getting ready to admit himself to hospital.

By the end of the shaving my pain had increased; by then I was crippled by the intensity of it. My father dressed me while my mother was on the phone to the ambulance. Because it was so early in the morning, they arrived at my home within minutes. As I was wheeled out to the ambulance, I called for my father. He was going to follow behind in his car while my mother travelled in the ambulance with me. I pulled him close and whispered, 'Bag my room, bag my room.' Then I passed out.

I was admitted to hospital by emergency ambulance for the second time. As I came to, I saw a bag of blood being pumped rapidly into the bulging vein of my arm. 'Matt, what are you doing back here my friend?' The voice of my caring doctor, with a very worried look on his face. He was standing by my bed in emergency, and my parents were once again cradling each other, with even more worried looks on their faces.

'Are you okay?' He continually asked questions—what was my name, date of birth, questions that would come naturally to your everyday person. I just nodded my head, I had no energy to talk. With each nod, my eyes closed; the doctor kept talking to me, to keep me awake and alert. But I was numb to his voice: the only thing I was aware of was pain—the pain in the right side of my stomach and the pain from a needle in my arm which felt like it had been inserted into my bone, that's how skinny I was at the time.

I was familiar with the feeling of a blood transfusion and the doctors didn't waste any time. They already knew my blood type and had it rushed to me. Apparently, my blood count was so low I was on the verge of being sent to the intensive care unit.

After an hour or so, a room became available. Throughout that night, I had a further three blood transfusions, with nurses monitoring me every half hour. By this time, my brother and sister-in-law had arrived; they were shocked to see me so close to death.

I don't remember much from that point; apparently a number of family and friends came to visit, but I don't remember seeing any of them. My energy levels were near non-existent so all I wanted to do was sleep.

I had lost a lot of weight over the months at home. I hadn't taken care of myself; you could feel and see my bones. My face had no colour; even with the blood transfusions I was in bad shape.

On the second morning, in walked the friendly doctor who wanted to check on my progress. He sat down and once again drew the curtains around, which was never a good sign. With my parents in the room, he sat on my bed and asked how I was. This time I had enough energy to reply with 'Fine.' 'Matt, I have got your blood results back from when you were admitted to emergency a few days ago. They show that not only have you had an ulcer flare up, you are actually suffering from pancreatitis.'

Pancreatitis, what is it? Had I been diagnosed with yet another disease—why not collect them and go for the trifecta? The doctor went on to explain about pancreatitis and its three possible causes: one is excessive drinking, two is your body not accepting medication, and three is unknown.

As I had assured my doctor that I had not been binge drinking, he assumed it had to be the result of my body rejecting the medication. So he decided to keep me in hospital under close observation, and treat me for the pancreatitis, continuing with blood and iron transfusions to replace the huge amounts I'd lost.

There was a little sigh of relief from everyone as the doctor left me with my family. I laid my head back down, looked over and there it was: my backpack. Dad had brought it from home, filled with clean clothes and other bits and bobs for me. My brother and sister-in-law took my mother outside for some fresh air, leaving my father and I alone. I looked over at him and thanked him for bringing my clothes, and asked what else he had packed for me. 'Matt, you packed the bag; you packed it with clean underwear, paper and pens, as though you knew you were coming here. You prepared it, I just brought it.'

In those early morning hours, somewhere along the line, I had packed my travel bag with appropriate items for a hospital stay; all before I went on to shave my body in the shower.

What sort of a mindset drives a person to prepare to go to hospital when in such pain that all they should be worried about is getting there? The funny thing was, I don't remember packing that bag, and I didn't know what was inside.

This time around, hospital was a little more comforting. I knew the procedures; I knew how the hospital system worked. So I adapted to it and made it work for me. Around the fifth day in, I once again started to show signs of life. I was sitting up in my bed, when my father looked at me and said, 'Son, is there anything I can get you?' I looked at him and said without a pause, 'A pen and paper.' 'Quickly, go and get it for him!' My mother urged my father to heed my request, as though I was about to write down the winning lottery numbers.

Here's the kicker … I was about to embark on a set of lifelong winning lottery numbers, that would take me out of the trenches, out of my dark times, and give me a sense of peace. And those winning numbers would be my art.

For the next few days and especially during the long nights when I was alone, I sketched like a madman. I drew religious images, angels, doves, anything with a positive message and I always captured the attention of the nurses.

It made me happy. I didn't talk much, my main form of communication was through my art. It was a connection to my soul. I started to give my sketches away and saw how happy it made people feel. In turn, that made me happy.

I was quickly recovering; talking, eating and walking again, pain free. It was a miracle. How could some ink and a pad rejuvenate a person, who only one week ago was near death?

After eleven days in hospital, the friendly doctor came to see me. He sat on my bed but this time didn't draw the curtains. He told me that I had made a quicker recovery than expected; the pancreatitis had been treated, my blood count was back up and the ulcers had gone down.

The only issue still remaining, and that needed to be attended to, was that I needed iron transfusions. But as these transfusions are lengthy and I could only have one a day, I could be released and come back once a week for the next eight weeks as an outpatient.

Without hesitation I agreed to his terms, with the biggest smile on my face. My mother and father quickly packed everything up, as we waited for my release papers. I was feeling great and, while I was waiting, I slowly went to the three elderly patients who shared my ward. I approached their families, then handed them all the same sketch, praying hands with rosary beads, that I had drawn especially for them.

I didn't care if they weren't religious; it wasn't a holy thing, it was a human thing. I wanted them to smile and feel happy and they did, each one hugging me, saying 'Thank you and God bless', filling me with a sense of joy.

'Matt, here are your papers. Now you have to promise me something: I want you to come and see me at my office, look after yourself, monitor your eating habits, and make sure you don't come back to hospital again. Promise me that, Matt?' 'I promise my friend.' I gave the friendly doctor a hug, grabbed my papers and slowly walked out of that hospital, knowing I would never allow myself to be in that state of health again.

During the next month, a new 'me' was born. I was alive again, having regular blood tests, seeing the caring doctor in his office. I had no pain, there was no blood and I had no sense of urgency to rush to the bathroom, all positive signs of no flare ups.

As promised, and really I had no choice, I had to make it back to the hospital once a week for my iron infusions. My father would drop me off and I would call him to pick me up after each session.

The iron always made me feel sick in the stomach but I could handle it. The room that the iron infusion took place was in a newly-renovated part of the hospital, everything was brand new and almost made you want to get sick to stay there. There were reclining chairs, you were served sandwiches and juice—they made it almost cool to be sick!

The room housed ten or so chairs and everyone was an outpatient of some sort. I never really chatted to anyone to learn their story; I always just took a pad and pen, and calming music to block everyone out, and would sketch away my three-hour sessions. Until the day it was the fifth session ...

I showed up as usual and the nursing staff greeted me, as they all knew who I was by then. There was no allocated seating, you could sit anywhere. There were only three people in the room at the time: an elderly man and two elderly ladies, perhaps all with an average age of sixty. One lady was sitting on the opposite side of the room by herself and I found myself drawn to her. Before I knew it, I was seated next to her.

Now it seemed as though this lady had light beaming out of her; she had a smile on her face from ear to ear and perhaps that's what drew me to her. I had no intention of talking to her but I found myself attracted by her warmth. I sat down and, within minutes, my shaved arm had the needle inserted, taped up and ready to go. After about fifteen minutes and a nice sandwich, the iron had started to enter my body.

By this stage I was usually blocked out from the world, drawing. But this time, as the river of iron flowed through my veins, I felt myself being drawn to this light, this elderly lady who was sitting next to me.

The room was usually dim but to my right was a light shining so brightly, I could not help but stare. I felt rude staring at this person next to me but I couldn't help it. I was just drawn to her and couldn't look away. The force of her light and positive energy drew my eyes back to her.

I tried to direct my eyes to something nearby, to alleviate the feeling of awkwardness she must have felt from me staring at her. I gazed up to see what was being dripped into this person's body. *Refrigerate, don't freeze* I read on the bag, written in big black font. As I gravitated my eyes back down, I noticed the lady was smiling directly at me.

I freaked out; should I say hello? Was she smiling at someone else, or was she smiling at me? I felt so awkward; my heart was racing, and I didn't know what to do or where to look.

I turned and looked the other way; she must have thought I was so rude. But, to be honest, I had no idea what was going on. Why was I so attracted to this person's energy and light? I couldn't wait for this iron session to be over.

I felt really bad. I am a friendly guy who always talks to people, especially the elderly, and here I was staring at someone I didn't know; and when she finally made eye contact with me I turned away, as if she had done something to offend me. What was wrong with me?

A few minutes later, as I finally regathered my thoughts and started to sketch again, the lady next to me and her aura started to shine even brighter, and my body began to tingle all over. I did everything in my power not to look at her this time around, but I knew that what was happening was not of this earth and could not be explained medically.

Once again, I found myself involuntarily turning my head in the direction of the lady to my right, who was beaming with light and positive energy. She slowly turned her head towards me; it was like she could sense when I was looking at her. This time I was prepared to say hello. She turned her head towards me and signalled for the nurse to come over. I thought she was going to ask to move seats, as there was a crazy young man staring at her.

The nurse approached the lady and I continued to draw, but all of my attention was on what was happening next to me. The nurse placed her ear near the lady's mouth and I heard her whisper, 'Please help me to the bathroom.'

I quickly turned away, sensing she needed some privacy, but still kept my peripheral vision on stand-by. The nurse removed the blanket from the elderly lady and, there it was, the most amazing beam of light and energy. The lady, who didn't stop smiling the whole time and who I was staring at uncontrollably, was revealed to have no legs and to be blind.

I was speechless and beside myself. I could have sworn this lady was talking to me through her eyes and, maybe she was. How could she have been so happy? Not only was she blind, she had no legs. How hard must life have been for her?

Only minutes later, my machine started to buzz. My iron infusion had finished, my drip was removed, and I shot out of there. I didn't see the old lady before I left, but something inside me knew that I had been meant to see her and experience her energy.

Was she an angel, was she God? She was something I needed to be shown by the higher source at that particular moment. All I know is I had never felt, until that point, such aura, energy and light beaming out of a human being.

Days after, I couldn't stop thinking about that lady. I even sketched her a few times, only her face, never anything else. I could never understand why or what happened; sometimes things don't need an explanation because they just happen and, if you feel peace from them, let them be.

I still question the experiences that transpired that day. Was that lady the beginning of my initiation into the spiritual and intuitive world? No doctors could explain the events that followed in the following months. I have kept some to myself until now, because the intensity was so high. I don't think even the most prepared person could explain the situations, sounds and experiences that my physical body would feel.

Chapter 13

Bless You

Thank you Lord, for this day.

Six months out of hospital I was feeling great. Every day I would wake up and say 'Thank you' out loud, just for being home and not in a hospital bed. I adopted an attitude of gratitude.

There was no blood loss, my weight was back to normal, I was regularly seeing the caring and happy doctor from the hospital, and I had found my passion for art again. I continued to practise art daily, just for myself. I was at peace.

There were only two issues: I was still on a lot of medication, which caused some side effects including heavy mood swings, reflux, nightmares and excessive weight gain. The second issue was that throughout my illness, my parents were the ones footing the bills for hospital visits, specialist appointments and medication.

I didn't have a lot of money at the time and I could see that my medical bills were taking a toll on my parents. They were paying for everything I needed and, being the kind-hearted people they are, they would never ask me to go and find work or pay for anything, after what I'd been through. Now that I was able to drive again and not worry about frequent bowel movements, it was time to set my sights back to the business world.

The entertainment world was long behind me; all of my contacts had been tarnished by my previous manager and that went for the candle, advertising and vending companies too. So I needed a creative, fresh, innovative, money-generating idea.

My energy levels were still too low to get involved in a nine to five. I knew I needed an entrepreneurial idea that would trump all of my others and make me far more money for doing less work. Then I'd be able to pay my parents back for what they had done for me.

But as experience illustrates, when you think about something too hard, the answer is never revealed. It's when you least expect it that little deposits are made or a light bulb moment happens, and that's exactly what happened to me.

Next day, a Thursday, I planned to go to the bank, to see how much damage had been done to my account and what I had left to invest into an existing company or a new business venture. This was my first big trip outside home. The bank was a half-hour drive and there were only two toilets on the way, so I needed to be careful.

On the way, I had no pains or urges to go to the bathroom, I felt great. As I drove into the car park, I felt a little pain and the urge to go. I quickly found a car space and ran quickly, but not too fast, to the closest bathroom. I made it to the toilet but, as I pulled down my pants, my stool was one step ahead of me and on its way out. It landed all over the toilet bowl and a little on my pants.

I didn't overreact this time as I'd travelled prepared: I wore dark pants and a woman's panty liner to absorb any blood loss.

I can remember when I first started to buy panty liners. I was in a state of panic in a shopping centre, bleeding, worried that it was showing through my underwear and about to seep into my jeans. So I thought, why not give them a try? And they worked! I didn't care, as long as I didn't bleed through my pants. I thought to myself at the time, what a great invention!

It was funny though, when I first bought them I was nervous. What would the cashier think of a guy buying women's panty liners? But, the quick thinker that I was, I decided to just say that they were for my girlfriend who wasn't feeling well. So each time I went to buy a packet or two or three, I would start the conversation by saying: 'How are you? Yep, I am a good boyfriend buying these for my girlfriend who's home in bed and not well.' Nine times out of ten, I would receive compliments, which eliminated any personal embarrassment.

I cleaned myself up almost as good as new, made my way to the bank, took my ticket and waited to be served. '89!' When my number was called, I jumped up and ran to the counter with my identification and account card and received my balance: $8,000.

Now for a lot of people that would have been devastating; after running multiple successful businesses with high profit margins, to have only $8,000 in the account rather than millions. But not for me—that was $8,000 I could use to get a business started.

What business I didn't know, all I knew was this time around I wanted to make a difference in this world. I wanted to create a business or maybe not necessarily create a business, just do something that would inspire people, help the silent sufferers and bring peace to this world.

I went to the toilet one last time before leaving the shopping centre to put my mind at ease for the journey ahead, then slowly drove home.

When I arrived home, I sat down with my mother for a cup of tea, explained my bank situation and we left it at that, just sitting in the moment. I think we both really didn't care about the money situation or what I was going to do for work, we were both happy to just be at home together. After a little while of peace I looked over to her and said,

'Mum, now that my health is well, what do you think I could do for work, to really enhance my life and, of course, help others?'

What happened next was a miracle; God's angels were in that room having a board meeting with us and we could feel it. Out of the blue my mother said, 'Why don't you go on stage and talk about your story? I am sure people would love to hear it.'

I instantly replied, 'I don't really like public speaking.' Then in the same breath I added, 'Maybe I could speak through my art?'

We were playing a verbal tennis match of creativity; the energy in the room was flowing and effortless. My mother returned with, 'Why don't you paint live on stage?' 'What would I paint?' 'Portraits' she said, 'Portraits of positive icons who have influenced this world in a positive way. But you have to do them BIG, almost life-size.' Then, all of a sudden, I found myself standing up looking at her, my hands in the air, shouting the following words:

'LET THE CANVAS SPEAK, LET THE CANVAS SPEAK!'

My mother and I both looked at each other as if to say, *What is happening right now?* But we knew the higher source was in play at that moment and there was no reason to question it; just go with it, it was divine intervention at its finest.

I ran to the garage, pulled out an old piece of canvas and just started to paint. Within minutes, my first portrait started to appear. I will never forget that moment, without thought I'd painted Michael Jackson, almost the same size as a standard household door.

My mother came out and couldn't believe her eyes; the angels continued to flow through us. My mother shouted, 'Paint it to music, that will add flow and movement, which will tie it all together!' So I did; using my experience from the entertainment industry, I implemented music, movement and art, combining them into one form of visual impact entertainment.

I spent the next month in my garage, practising various portraits— Mother Teresa, Jesus, Gandhi. Throughout that time, I kept having flashbacks of my hospital experience drawing for people and the joy it gave them, and it made me smile. I had no idea what I was going to do with this, all I knew was that it felt right, so I continued to practise and develop my own personal style.

Two months of solid practice later, my father came home from work one evening. I had set the garage up like a mini theatre with two chairs and I'd even made refreshments. I sat my parents down and didn't say a word, just smiled. I pressed play and, to the sound of *Billie Jean*, painted Michael Jackson's portrait. Within a matter of minutes, there was Michael Jackson, staring right back at my parents.

I will never forget that day. The song had finished, I had just completed the portrait, I was dripping with sweat and there was paint everywhere, even on my mum. I gazed over at my parents, waiting for a reaction. After two minutes of silence, which felt like an hour, I broke the silence with 'AND?' My parents both stood up, burst into tears and just hugged me; my mother held me close and whispered, 'Bless you.' I knew there and then I had found my inspiration, and my inspiration had found me.

What I wasn't aware of was the path I was about to pave: a new life, career and experiences. But best of all, I would meet and inspire people, through what had conspired between my mother and me. To this day, we still just look at each other and smile, knowing we were in spirit on the day I was reborn and found my purpose.

Being the businessman that I am, I still didn't know how I was going to get this new form of inspiration out into the world. I knew there would be costs involved, but I was almost sure it was not going to cost anywhere near the $8,000 I had left.

After a night's worth of mind mapping, I came up with a rough business plan and costs involved. I had decided to continue with the inspirational speaker theme my mother had originally suggested, but somehow to go on stage at events and incorporate my art, while talking about my story. With that concept in mind, I knew what would be needed to produce such a stage show—not very much at all.

I would need carpet to cover the floor wherever I performed; an industrial canvas stand, as the portraits I would be painting would be of large scale; paint, brushes, canvas, buckets, rags and toolboxes; and it all had to be lightweight and mobile. It had to be lightweight and mobile because there was a divine knowing within that what I was about to embark on was big and was going to be global, so whatever I constructed needed to be a global travelling enterprise.

With that thought in mind I went to work, sketching up the stage show set-up for my performance. After a day or so I had the visual, with all of the materials needed written on the side of the illustration mock-up. I then researched each item; where I could purchase them and how much each item would cost. Everything I needed was a one-off purchase, except for canvas and paints; they would be my only ongoing costs.

The following week, after I had worked out costs and drawn up the final sketch, I presented the information to my parents, as though they were my angel investors and I was pitching my million-dollar idea. In a sense they were my angel investors. I think we all knew I was onto something big, especially my mother, who really was my co-creator. But as I'd found in the past, it's always a good move to illustrate to your business partners, in this case my parents and saviours, the business plan with its risks and rewards.

Over dinner that night, I showed them my foolproof plan with materials needed. Costs amounted to $2,500 which I easily had.

My plan was to share my story at events and, at the end of each event, I would paint just as I did for my parents that day in the garage. I would paint someone who is or has been an inspiration to the world, leaving my audience captivated and speechless. They would watch someone who had gone from a hospital bed to the world stage, turning a blank canvas into a portrait in a small amount of time. It all sounded perfect.

Then my father hit me with a very important question that I'd overlooked: 'Matt, this all sounds great, it's inspiring. You get to do what you love, your art, and share your story with people, hopefully helping them in their own personal journey. But how will you get your gigs and who will you perform and speak to?'

That was a great question. I had worked out all of the equipment I needed, how much it would all cost, I'd even worked out a brief script and a list of icons I could paint. The one element of this genius plan that I neglected to think about was who I would bring this show to.

This stopped me in my tracks for a moment. I couldn't call on my old contacts within the entertainment industry, those relationships and bridges had been burnt, and not by my own doing.

So in my mind that eliminated most of the corporate venue market. I was drawing a blank, which was quite unusual for me, especially within the business arena, where I was quite the troubleshooter.

After my father asked that ever so important question, I sat back down on my dining chair with a look of confusion on my face. I continued to eat in silence, allowing my brain to work on a possible solution. All I knew was that, despite this hurdle, there was no way I was going to give in easily. This performance concept had been delivered to my mother and me in a way that could not have been of this world. It was meant to be and I had to find a way.

I set out next day to purchase all the materials I needed to perform. Luckily, almost everything was available from the one industrial-type warehouse store. All of the materials were delivered to me that afternoon. I still didn't have a concrete plan regarding who I was going to perform in front of, but I was confident, knowing that the universe would send the answer my way soon enough.

I knew what I needed next: a business name to really capture people's attention. Something that would express inspiration, art and my story, all in a short phrase. I spent hours experimenting with different words and phrases but they didn't feel right.

Once again, my mother came into my room at just the right time, to ask if I wanted something to eat. She could see the frustration in my face and asked what was wrong. 'Mum, I need a name for what I am doing; something that will capture people's attention and express my story, my art and inspiration in the one business name. It's so hard.'

Mum looked at me and smiled. I looked back and knew something was happening, something of the spiritual realm again. 'Matteo Charles.' Mum said it again, 'Matteo Charles.' Then she followed with, 'Your name is all you need, son. Matteo means 'gift of God' and your name is everything you need; your story, your art, your gifts, your inspiration— Matteo Charles.' Then she left my room.

A feeling of peace flowed through my body. She was right; my name expressed everything, all I had been through and where I was going. I added the simple words 'inspirational artistry' and *Matteo Charles Inspirational Artistry* was born!

I quickly checked whether the domain and business names were available. They were, so I swiftly registered both. Next I needed a logo, something that would again represent my journey. I knew what I wanted, so feeling inspired (or in spirit), I sketched out a rough version of what I saw my logo to be.

In one's life there are just a handful of people that you can call true friends. Sometimes 'true friend' is an understatement—'undercover angel' is probably a better description.

I have one such friend to this day. He is a graphic designer I met back when I was a corporate DJ, and he was the MC for most of the weddings I played at. We connected instantly and became firm friends. When we first met, I asked him to design some DJ cards and he never charged me for it. I was very grateful but always felt bad and wanted to repay him somehow.

During almost fifteen years of friendship, this person has designed all of my company logos, flyers and marketing material and has never charged me a cent. He has helped me so much and his friendship is something I hold dear to my heart. Every time he designed something for me, he nailed the brief without any need for changes from my end. He is a true friend and professional.

The Matteo Charles logo design process was no different. I called him and ran through exactly what I needed. He could hear the excitement in my voice and asked me to email what I had already sketched. In less than a day, the logo was sent back to my inbox and, once again, he had nailed exactly what I had envisioned. *Matteo Charles Inspirational Artistry* was staring right back at me, and I could not have been more inspired.

The set-up was now sitting in my garage; all of the tools had been purchased, the canvas and paints bought, the logo and business name designed, and freshly-made business cards were ready to hand out. The only problem was that I had no idea how I was going to present my new form of inspiration to the world.

But as I have found in the past, signs are revealed to us in the least obvious ways. Sometimes we need to travel the most undesired path, to reach the smoothest of journeys. And that's exactly what I was about to be exposed to, after all the years of abuse, early business ventures, severe illness, and almost leaving this earth. All were on the path to finding my true purpose, living my passion and spreading my wings, to really live the life I was intended to. I just didn't realise how high my angel wings were going to take me.

Chapter 14

Art and Soul

Mum and Dad, the hard work is done. I have designed the logo, registered the business name, bought all of the equipment and practise every day in the garage. I just have to find somewhere to perform.

'Son, let it find you,' my mum would reply. She was right; up until that point my purpose had found me, so why interrupt the process? I was anxious to expose my form of expression to the world, to see the reaction from others to confirm that this was my true purpose.

About two weeks of daily eight-hour portrait practise sessions later, I felt really sick. There were small trickles of blood when I went to the bathroom, and I couldn't work out why. My diet was much healthier, my energy levels were where they needed to be, and my sleep patterns were much better.

One particular night I was really tired and in a lot of pain. I had done a lot of painting that day, so my eyes were crusty and tired. It was about nine o'clock, my parents had gone to bed and I was staring at the television screen, hoping the picture would help me doze off.

I switched off the television and decided to try and get some proper sleep. I walked past the kitchen, which housed all of my medication. I needed to take my last batch of tablets for the day but, for some reason,

I decided not to and went straight to bed. For the first time in a very long time, I fell straight into a deep sleep.

Little did I know, that deep sleep was about to propel me into a world and experience that my family still speaks about to this day.

I remember it as though it were yesterday. I was fast asleep; all of a sudden a light was glowing at my bedroom door. I always slept with my door closed, which didn't make a lot of sense as my parents' room was on the floor above.

This wasn't a bright light; there was just enough light to see if someone was walking towards me. All of a sudden the room started to fill with smoke. And then he appeared, a little boy with a crew cut hairstyle, big black eyes and no legs—the smoke was his legs—and he started to glide towards me.

As he approached my bed, I could see he was holding an object with both hands close to his chest. At this point I realised I was seeing all of this unfold very slowly, through a third eye. I was having the most surreal out-of-body experience and I was watching everything unfold through that third eye. I was witnessing a devil-like child floating towards me with a knife. Only I could save myself. But how, when I was watching myself sleep and this child was almost at my bedside with his knife and smoke-like legs? How could I be a spectator and player at the same time?

Within a split second, the 'sleeping me' heard the 'watching me' speak, muttering these words in a calm, angelic voice: 'Matt, roar! Roar as loud as you can! Don't scream; roar like a lion and he will go.'

I was fast asleep, yet I knew and felt exactly what was going on. Then, outside my control, the boy was an inch away from me. I remember roaring so loudly I could feel my chest inflate from the immense pressure and, just like that, he was gone; he floated away, the room emptied of smoke and the light disappeared.

I didn't wake up once during that night, even though I knew everything that had happened, through the eyes of the person sleeping and my higher self.

The next morning I woke up, feeling quite at ease. I found my parents sitting on the lounge, pale as if they'd seen a ghost. 'What's wrong with you two?' I greeted them with. 'Didn't you hear what happened last night?' my mother asked, going on to explain that there had been a huge car accident in the early hours of the morning, right in front of our house, and a little boy had died. But an hour prior to the accident, they'd heard such a loud scream, they thought someone was in their room. They'd rushed downstairs to check on me and found me fast asleep. Then an hour later, the car accident occurred. The ambulance and police were called and I had slept through the entire thing.

I paused and replayed in my mind what my mother had just told me. All I had registered was that a little boy had died and my parents had heard a roar-like scream. 'Matt, what's wrong?' my mother asked me, as she noticed my puzzled look. 'Mum, was the scream like a roar, like a lion-type roar?' 'Yes Matt, it was. It was very loud and disturbing; did you hear it too?' Without making a big deal of it, I looked at my parents and said, 'Oh yeah, that was me. I saw myself being attacked by a devil-like child holding a knife, and the only way to be saved was to roar. So I did.' I walked off and started to make breakfast.

That incident was never brought up again; it was as though there was a knowing from both of my parents not to say anything. That moment was to be known and heard by the three of us but never spoken about again.

That experience opened my spiritual side to a world that can only be experienced, not explained. What had happened was not of the physical world, and would become ever so present in my life in the coming years.

It was Monday morning, the start of a new week, and a night away from my screaming moment that had so scared my parents. I had a specialist appointment, I was feeling quite good, and had taken a blood test the week prior, a necessary procedure the week before my check-ups.

I entered the doctor's office feeling confident and happy, I'd arrived without having to stop to use a bathroom. I had no pains and felt like Superman, not to mention I was inspired as I waited daily for the universe to illustrate the next move for my art venture.

'Welcome Matt, please come in.' I had a good relationship with my specialist; I didn't get too close personally, but close enough for him to tell me things off the record. I gave him a watered-down version of my new business venture. He could clearly see that I was in a good space mentally, which made what he was about to tell me a little easier.

He opened my file which contained a whole bunch of numbers and scientific names that I really didn't care about; all I needed to know was how my blood levels were; as for the rest, I wasn't interested. He presented me with my blood tests and illustrated that they weren't too good. He went on to explain that I was currently inflamed and that I should be hospitalised immediately to get on top of it.

But there was a twist ... my specialist couldn't work out why I wasn't hurled over in pain with such low blood levels. He asked how I was honestly feeling, and I told him: I was great, no pain that day, no sick feeling in my stomach, I felt like a new person.

For a minute I stepped back from the situation, I guess another out–of-body moment, and thought to myself: *How could this person who has had the highest of education, studied in a specialist field and assessed multitudes of people with the same condition, not be able to work out why I wasn't fitting into his textbook diagnosis?*

He looked at me with a puzzled expression, not saying a word, just continually feeling my pulse. At that point, something inside me realised that I wasn't a medical subject. I wasn't what these doctors had labelled me: *a disease*. I was a human being, someone made up of billions of particles of energy. I was not formed in a lab and would not be controlled by one. I was an extension of the highest source and no-one would take that away from me, especially now.

'Look Matt, you say you're physically well. You don't seem to be in pain or running to the bathroom, but the data shows otherwise. I am rather baffled. What I can and want to suggest is, instead of admitting you back into hospital, starting you on a drug, but it comes with conditions. This particular drug is usually given in a hospital, so I would need you to come back to me every single day so I can check on your progress. There are also some major side effects, one being that if you ever decide to have children, this particular drug could cause your child to be retarded.'

I could not believe what I was hearing; my blissful mood instantly changed and I started to feel rage. I kept quiet, didn't say a word, simply continued to listen to this person who was trying to take over my body and put something inside it that was a disease of its own. Sure, it would have stopped the bleeding, and momentarily stopped my periodic pains but, in return, I would develop every other disease in the book.

I was so angry I was about to storm out of the room, but I knew better. I agreed to what he was saying, so that I could get out of that room. I collected my prescription and the paperwork about the side effects of this so-called 'wonder pill' and drove home.

I drove home that day feeling so angry, confused and emotional. I thought to myself: How do we humans allow other humans, who have two letters at the start of their name representing the word 'doctor', to take our lives into their hands, when really the only person who should be responsible for our lives is ourselves.

I'd had enough; I wasn't a lab rat for doctors to trial things on and work out why I was such a rare case. I had suffered too much and lost too much to go through it all again. That day a switch was flicked on within me; I like to describe it today as the 'motivation vs. inspiration switch'.

Motivation gets you excited; when you go to a wealth or educational seminar, watch a movie or hear a song, you get motivated, but the motivation only lasts for a short amount of time, usually only hours after the event you attended or witnessed. By the next day, you have usually forgotten most of what you saw, as you return to your everyday routine.

Inspiration, however, is so much stronger. Inspiration flicks a switch within, as though it takes the blinkers off your eyes. You become set on a mission, not just for a day, a month or a year—it's a lifelong mission. You need to keep going until you find answers but, even when the answers are found, you want to learn from them in your own way and then go on to teach others what you have learnt, handing over the baton of inspiration in that particular field.

Driving home from the specialist that day I was inspired, not from a positive influence but from anger. I wanted to take control of my life again. I'd had enough of this so-called disease controlling me and doctors pointing my life in the direction they wanted me to live. My inspiration was to take control of my life again and be the one in the driver's seat.

If I truly wanted to inspire people through my art and my story, I needed to take my life back into my own hands there and then. When I arrived home that day, I stormed inside, turned on my laptop, and was on a mission. For the first time since I had been diagnosed, I was about to start a crash course on the disease itself, and research individual cases on the same medications. But there was one particular area that I wanted to know and research more than anything.

Instead of just researching people who were living with the same disease, I wanted to research, know, learn and contact people who had been diagnosed with the same disease but had cured themselves from it naturally, with no medication. People who had stepped out on a limb and made a leap of faith … they were the ones I wanted to know about.

Day and night, I searched web page after web page. I sent hundreds, even thousands, of emails to people who had overcome the disease. I wanted to know them and know how. If they could do it, why couldn't I?

Finally the breakthrough came. One morning I woke up after a long night of research and went straight to my emails, to see if I'd had any replies from the previous night. There it was, a reply from an American man, whose story I had come across on the internet.

He had been diagnosed with Ulcerative Colitis, and had gone through numerous emergency hospital treatments, as had I. He had been on the same medications, but his condition had been worse than mine, to the point where doctors basically told him that he had to have his bowel removed, due to the amount of scarring and damage caused by the active ulcers. Out of sheer desperation, he took to the web to find people who had cured themselves. Now his way of repaying the world was to reply to me, as someone had once done for him.

I immediately emailed him back, thanking him for his reply. I asked if we could chat over the phone, supplying my phone number to see whether this guy was for real and if he would call me from overseas. To my surprise, fifteen minutes later my phone rang and he was at the other end.

For the next five hours, I spoke to someone on the other side of the world who I had never met. I poured out my heart to him. Looking back now it was quite risky, this guy could have been anyone, but that wasn't on my mind. My mind was full of hope, holding on for the pain to end. I needed to end the vicious cycle of pain I was living with and I needed to end it now.

At the end of our conversation I thanked him so much for calling; I can't imagine how much his phone call would have cost. He ended the call by saying he was going to send me a manual that he had written and that he was about to publish globally for other Ulcerative Colitis sufferers. He wanted me to have it now, so I could start the process straight away. He told me that I would see rapid results in just three weeks. That was hard for me to believe, as I had been suffering for years, but I was willing; I had made it this far and couldn't turn back now.

There were two elements that he stressed: that this had worked for him but may not work for me, as each person is different; also that if I was to embark on this venture I needed to stop all medications, as they would interfere with the healing process.

That was music to my ears. I hated my medication and its side effects; I had poor sleep, my weight fluctuated weekly, I would constantly get angry or depressed. This was a no-brainer for me. But I knew it was going to be a problem for two other people who didn't see life through my eyes, and they were my parents.

We hung up the phone and I waited for the email containing his manual, a rush of excitement, nervousness and fear racing through my body. There it was—one unread email with attachment. It was such a large file it took a while for it to download. As it was downloading I told myself that I had to have my parents on board because, if I didn't, I would not only be battling this new lifestyle but I would also be battling their disapproval and I just didn't need that.

I walked out of my bedroom to see my parents both watching television. I asked them to join me at the dining table, which was always a sign

I wanted to talk. I explained what had happened at the specialist a few days earlier and what I had been doing since. It didn't take me long to break down in tears, pleading with them to be on my side. I'd experienced enough pain and needed them to trust me and what I wanted for my life and for myself.

It took hard talk and a lot of crying from the three of us, but eventually they gave in. 'Okay Matt, you know what you are doing. We trust you, we hate to see you in pain, do this your way. We aren't happy about you stopping your medication but that's something we will have to live with for now. But, if you don't improve, you will go back to the specialist, okay?'

I readily agreed. Now that I had my parents' approval, it was the beginning of my new life; but I needed them to know I wasn't joking and was more than serious.

What I did next made things quite real for my parents, and exciting for me. I got up from the kitchen table and headed towards the medicine cabinet. I placed all four bottles of medication on the kitchen bench. I could see my parents looking at me and probably thinking: *Didn't he just tell us he wasn't taking his medication anymore?* But I wasn't about to take my medication, I was about to get rid of it all for good.

I grabbed the dishwashing detergent and removed the lids from the containers of medicine. Then I poured detergent into them one by one, until they were filled to the brim.

My parents watched on in silence. When I reached the final one I said out loud, as though I was performing some ritual of my own, 'This day marks the day of no more medication; let thy body be thy chemist, let thyself heal within!' Then I closed the lid of every bottle of medicine and threw them in the bin.

I can remember that exact moment. I closed my eyes at the very end and felt a wave of calmness. I stopped shaking, my tears dried, and happiness radiated through my body. I closed the bin, walked to my room, opened the completed document download from my new American friend and devoured that book, as though it was the Bible handed down from Jesus to his disciples. Looking back on it now, it kind of was.

I believe that in life everything happens for a reason. Sometimes we don't get to know or understand that reason immediately; sometimes it is thrown right in our faces and other times we are meant to work it out for ourselves.

That time in my life was make or break time for me. I had developed a new performance that I was inspired to share with the world, but I knew within that I could not fulfil that journey until my health was 110%. I needed to be at optimum health.

For the next two weeks, I implemented the first section of the plan. It consisted of freshly-made raw organic juices eight times a day, and that was it. I was to eat no solids, and especially no animal products. Every day, I had to be exposed to the sun for twenty-five minutes, do fifteen minutes of light exercise of my choice and, most importantly, do three things that made me happy.

The detox was hard for me. I loved coffee, I liked to eat meat, and really didn't enjoy having raw, juiced products. But if I wanted to improve my health, I had to fight the urge of temptation harder than ever. The aim of this part of the program was to alkalise your body, as disease cannot live in an alkalised environment.

Sitting in the sun each morning was heaven; I would sit by the pool with my shirt off, embracing the sun heating up my body with natural medicine. As for finding three things that made me happy beyond belief, I only needed art. It released my soul from the world and connected my true being to its natural source of peace.

The second part of the program was to keep a diary of what juices I'd had daily, whether they had reacted with my stomach and, if so, determine what ingredient reacted with me most and eliminate that immediately. Combined with that, I needed to record how many times I was going to the bathroom. At the start of the detox, I was going to the bathroom at least seven times a day. But the movements were easy, there was no pressure, so I wasn't coming out of the toilet as though I had run a marathon. It was all happening naturally, without force and pain.

My American friend was right. After just three weeks, my energy levels were through the roof. I was up early, my room was spick and span, I was a new person. I was going to the bathroom once a day, if that, and I was excited to see what juice I was going to have that day.

By that time, I had successfully made it through the hardest point of the program. I constantly kept in contact with my American friend, who was just as keen to see the results as I. The next step was to continue the juicing eight times a day, but now implement a small piece of solid food into my diet. It had to be raw: fruit, vegetable, or a type of nut. It was a trial and error system, to see which foods worked with my own internal system.

I felt amazing; my sleep patterns were regular and peaceful. I would fall asleep every night about nine and wake up at six in the morning. My parents couldn't believe their eyes and, the best thing, my art was flowing like never before. It was like I was creating from the soul, without thought. It was art and soul at its best; it was heaven.

For the first time in years, I was living an abundant life and I was not about to lose it. I continued to follow my program of daily fresh juices, natural sun, solid raw meals, indulging in my passions (mostly art), blocking out all negative outside energy, including people and all portals of media.

I continued to study natural healing and found out that acupuncture was great for blood flow and increased energy. I was familiar with the Eastern way of life from my martial arts days.

If you study Asian and Eastern medicine philosophies, almost all of their healing properties are natural and that fitted perfectly into my new lifestyle. I continued my journey further with weekly acupuncture, acupressure and Tai Chi sessions. I even did meditation classes, to help with my anxiety and connect me to my spiritual side more closely.

I was into my third month of the program. I felt at near optimum health, you could say I was reborn. During my personal healing months, I was contacted by my specialist, but one of my conditions was that I was not to be contacted by any medical professionals. I didn't care who it was; if they called, my parents were to tell them I was overseas and would be in contact with them on my return.

But the time had come and I was ready to see him; I wanted to be tested to see how my natural plan would be read in terms of medical results. 'Matt, where in the world have you been? You had me worried.' I had made an appointment to see my specialist, to schedule a colonoscopy. My American friend stressed the fact that, if I stuck with the program, not only would it 'cure' my disease, it would actually reverse it. The scarring from my ulcers in the lining of my bowel would actually disappear and, to prove it, I was to have a colonoscopy procedure. My specialist was more than happy to oblige, as he hadn't seen me in months and wanted to know what was going on.

Two days later I was booked in for a colonoscopy. The hardest thing about this particular procedure is that you have to drink the worst bowel-cleaning drink known to man. It was horrible; it had to be mixed with about three litres of water and drunk twelve hours before the procedure. It tasted like slime.

A colonoscopy used to knock me about; the anaesthetic always reacted badly with me, making me very drowsy and tired for days after. I was always booked to go and see the specialist the following day and this time was no exception. However, the results came with a twist this time.

My father picked me up from the day surgery where the colonoscopy had taken place and I was in my drowsy phase. When we arrived home, my mother was at the door waiting for us with a big smile on her face. She ran out to greet me and gently walked me inside. I wanted to go straight to sleep and thought she was going to tuck me into bed. However, as I entered the kitchen, there was my specialist! It was only a few hours before that I had seen him, just before he was about to stick a camera down my throat and in my rear. The question was, what was he doing in my kitchen and so quickly after the procedure?

That day was one of the happiest days of my life, not only because of the information I received sitting around the kitchen table with my father, mother and my specialist. It was also because, for once in my life, I had self-respect. I had listened to myself and hadn't allowed anyone, whether a boss, doctor or anyone in authority, to abuse me and be careless with my life. For once, I'd taken control of my own life; going against the current had paid off.

My specialist could not believe the photos he was showing us of my bowel. They were as though from a different person, no sign of any ulcers, no inflammation but, most amazing of all and what had him baffled the most, the scarred tissue within my bowel had mostly healed from within.

'Matt, what happened? How did this happen, you must tell me?' My specialist was never going to get the answer out of me, not because I didn't want him to know, but because I knew he wouldn't understand and would have wanted to take further tests to make sure this result was correct. I knew they were correct and the proof was there for all to see. I walked over to him, put my hand on his shoulder and said, 'Do you really want to know what happened, Doc?' 'Of course' he replied, with his eyebrows raised so high I thought they were going to get caught in his hair. 'Well Doc, I never wanted to see you again!' I smiled, gave him a pat on the shoulder, walked to my room and had the most peaceful sleep I'd had to date.

I never went back to that specialist; well, not as a patient. I still email him every couple of months and he jokingly asks when I am going to reveal my magic secret. I always reply with a spiritually-driven answer, intended to send his thoughts in a frantic direction.

I continued on my natural diet. I'd eat a piece of organic or grain-fed meat every few months, to satisfy the small craving I had. The same with coffee or any other naughty food I used to enjoy eating, but I have always been directed back to the program that saved my life.

My passion for art only became stronger and my one true mission was to get my story out for the world to hear and see. With art, I knew there was a greater purpose; I had just been too fearful to give it a go in the past. But now was the time to pursue my life's purpose: to create a platform that would engage people like nothing else.

As for my American friend, I never did meet him. After my three-month program and its positive results, I never heard from him again. He never replied to my emails; I even tried calling him a few times with no answer.

I always think about him in a positive light. I am a little upset that I never got to thank him in person. But I often find myself sitting in the sun thinking about him or about the real-life angel the Lord sent to heal my pain. I always feel a sense of peace, knowing that I was touched by something not many will experience. What was opened internally for me was something that words could not explain, only feelings within could illustrate. All I knew was that pain was behind me and the greatest canvas of all was about to be painted.

Chapter 15

There's Art in Greatness

Good morning Dad, let's go and see how the bonsais have grown overnight.

One hobby my dad holds dear to his heart is growing and caring for bonsai trees. He enjoys the entire process; whenever he is trimming or talking to them it seems as though he is at peace.

'So Dad, I haven't told Mum yet but guess what? I have my first art performance gig this weekend!'

I'd received an email from an old friend, a much older guy I'd met back when I was growing all of my companies. He had helped me secure a large national advertising contract for my vending machines. To be honest, I was surprised he was still talking to me after my little empire had come crashing down, as he had been the referral for advertising in my business. Usually, when someone recommends you in business and the deal goes sour, that person ceases their relationship with you, as you have tarnished their name. But this case was different and we became very close over the years. He even came to visit me in hospital a few times; he was quite the gentleman.

He was a very wealthy middle-aged man; most of his wealth had been generated through property development. I had met with him a week prior for lunch, where we celebrated me overcoming my health hurdles.

But as per usual, when you meet with someone who is like-minded, even if your aim is to talk general conversation, I knew business would come up one way or another.

He asked what was next for me; by then I had created a basic website and recorded a video of me painting Einstein. I had thought to myself: *I could explain to people what I did, or what I wanted to do, but in this visually-driven world it's so much easier to show people.* Hence the video.

The video was made professionally and came out exactly the way I wanted. I had performed to inspirational music, to enhance the emotional feeling of the video. It had been edited and played for just under three minutes. It seemed the ideal time to show someone from outside my circle what I wanted to do in life, to get their reaction and opinion.

I pulled out my phone, brought up the video and pressed play. I sat back in my chair, watching his facial expressions throughout the video without making it too obvious. 'So what did you think?' The video had ended and I needed to know his thoughts. 'Have you performed this anywhere else?' 'Not yet, do you know anywhere or anyone having an event I can perform at?' 'Are you confident about this Matt? I mean can you execute a large portrait in under ten minutes to music without fail?' 'I sure can,' I swiftly replied.

Then to my surprise he hit me with, 'Okay Matt, this Saturday I am holding a charity event at my home for 200 people. It's a black tie event and the theme is rock and roll.' Immediately I thought of two identities I could paint: Elvis and Sinatra. But before I could suggest my two identities he said, 'I want you to paint Elvis and Sinatra. I know there will be people at the event who love those two identities. They have deep pockets and should pay big for them, if they are painted and executed right.'

Once again, I knew the universe was speaking to me. There was no doubt in my mind I could execute both of those identities, in under ten minutes each. I was familiar with the layout of his house; it was huge, so there would be no problem with performance space area. The only thing we had not spoken about was my fee, but I knew it would come into play soon enough.

Now that wasn't a big deal to me. I knew that if I performed at this event and mesmerised his crowd with what I was born to do, I would have no problems selling each piece and, most importantly, securing further work.

So with that in mind I needed to be strategic. I proposed the idea of not charging a fee at all to perform. I would paint both Elvis and Sinatra as promised and we would auction them live on the night. Whatever money was raised; he would keep 100% of for his charity.

How my remuneration worked was simple; I would paint a third piece, a portrait of my choice, and I would keep 100% of whatever that sold for. He smiled, shook my hand and, within an hour, I had my first live performance art gig.

After explaining the situation to my father over our bonsai bonding session, I headed inside to tell my mother the whole story again. My parents were both very happy for me; they couldn't understand why I wasn't charging a performance fee but I urged them to trust me, as I knew this was going to work out perfectly.

On the following Saturday night, just one week after I had secured my first art performance show, and only a few months after gaining a great bill of health, I felt at peace and at ease for the first time in a long time.

I spent most of the night in the guesthouse, adjacent to where the party was happening. It was important to keep me hidden so my performance would be a surprise for the guests.

I was to perform at nine, my stage and materials were ready and waiting. I had arrived before the guests to set everything up, placing a black sheet over the entire set-up, so guests wouldn't know what was happening.

I don't think the wife of my wealthy friend was too happy about me being there, as all she saw was paint and paintbrushes on stage. I am sure her immediate thoughts were she didn't want this skinny kid spilling paint all over her multi-million-dollar home! I assured her I would be very careful and there was nothing to worry about.

It was 8.50pm, ten minutes before show time. I could hear the MC gathering everyone around the pool, for the secret performance that was about to take place. At that time, I didn't have any credentials of past performances, so I wrote a brief description of who I was and how I came to be in front on them that evening, including an introduction for the MC to use.

As I made my way to the stage to begin this important shift in my life, I had a surreal moment. Just as I had done before my first major DJ gig and each time I returned home from hospital, I looked up and just said 'Thank you'.

I floated back to reality, heard the crowd clapping and made my debut as a live performance painter. To be honest, I don't remember being in the moment performing that night. It was as though I had blanked out during my performance; I had no thoughts, no fear, no anxiety and was truly in spirit.

Within half an hour I had completed three paintings: Elvis, Sinatra and Marilyn_Monroe. I chose Marilyn for my third painting, as research showed she was among the most famous icons that have passed, along with Elvis and Sinatra.

As soon as my performance was over, the music stopped. I had high fived my last painting with paint on my hand, a signature move I do, to let people know I have finished a piece. As I high fived my last piece, the canvas of Marilyn Monroe, I turned around to look at the crowd to express my gratitude. There was total silence.

My heart dropped to the floor. There I was, standing with paint all over me, sweating like crazy, a smile painted on my face, thinking that these people absolutely hated me. As the MC made his way over to thank me for my performance, I turned away and started putting lids back on the paint cans. I was broken. I didn't want anyone to see the disappointment on my face, especially my wealthy friend.

All of a sudden one person started to clap, then two people, then ten. I turned around and there was a sea of cameras snapping like crazy, the entire crowd was screaming, cheering and clapping, and it went on for a full two minutes.

I was in shock; I couldn't believe it. I stopped packing up my paints, stood up, turned round and stared back at the crowd, smiling and waving my hands in gratitude.

But the true test would be the sale of each piece. With the crowd still in their cheering and clapping frenzy, I knew I had to capitalise on the feelings of these potential buyers. So I whispered to the MC, 'Start the auction now. Don't waste time, do it **now!**'

Thankfully, the MC was a switched-on businessman, he was actually a real estate auctioneer as I came to learn after the auction had ended. He knew what I meant; he knew we had to impulse sell and have the buyers outbidding each other there and then. And that's exactly what he did.

That night my first two paintings—one of Elvis and the other of Sinatra—sold for $25,000 each. As for Marilyn, well she sold for $45,000. That's right, and I kept her entire sale price!

The night was a huge success. I spent the remainder of the party networking, having photos taken with people, handing out my new business cards, and feeling like a superstar.

Driving home that night, I was in another world. I laughed, I cried, a million emotions raced through my soul. It wasn't because of the fat cheque I had in my wallet or because people had embraced my performance. It was that I finally understood ... I finally understood that everything that I had gone through since leaving high school, as a blank canvas ready to be painted on, had led me to that evening and I finally got it.

The next morning, I woke up around ten, quite exhausted from the emotional roller-coaster of the night before. I found my parents watching TV, anxiously waiting to hear about the night before. 'Well Matt, how did it go?' my mother asked. I smiled at her and handed her an envelope containing the cheque for $45,000. Before she could open it, I walked off, looking back to ask, 'I am making a cup of tea. Would anyone like one?'

I hadn't realised that many of the 200-strong VIPs at my wealthy friend's party sat on boards of charities and major companies or were business owners. My life's purpose was about to come to fruition; doors were about to open for me to perform internationally, and in front of world leaders.

During my first year as a performance painter, I was booked out twice a week, almost every week. Performing at charity events around the country, I sometimes found myself talking to the audience about my story and how I came to be standing in front of them. My story always amazed the crowd left them wanting to know more.

One of the most memorable charity events involved the opportunity to paint world-renowned talk show host Sir Michael Parkinson live. Sir Michael then signed the painting and the charity sold it live that night.

I was finally living my purpose, full steam ahead, and it wasn't about to stop. For over a year, I worked at various charity events and even performed on popular TV shows, including *X Factor Australia*, where I painted singer Guy Sebastian as he debuted his latest single. I was interviewed on Sydney's leading radio station and featured in many print and online publications. And I was about to receive an email that would take me global.

An email had arrived from an international wellness festival, inviting me to perform a number of paintings and speak at the *Wanderlust NZ and Australia Festival* in early 2015. *Wanderlust* festivals had a good reputation so I was very interested. After a few back and forth emails, I had secured my first international performance gig.

So by late 2014 I was living my purpose and spreading inspiration through my unique platform of live art. I truly felt that nothing was impossible. Up until that point, everything that had happened within the art arena had been effortless and had just come to me. I truly felt it was through divine intervention, so I had been content to continue down that path.

But now, as a strong believer of the universe's plan and of affirmations, I decided to write down a few goals that I wanted to reach by mid-2015. One was that I wanted to collaborate with a reputable global company; it didn't matter who, as long as the brand stood for the same morals and inspirational journey that I was on. I wanted to design something to fit in with their product range, have my artwork integrated into that product and for it to be made available globally.

Another goal was more unrealistic but I believed in it so much, there was no way it could not come to fruition.

During my time in hospital, there was one thing, other than drawing, that would bring me peace. Using my smart phone, I used to watch videos of spiritual leaders and teachers that I found a connection with:

Dr. Wayne Dyer, Deepak Chopra, Anthony Robbins, Bruce Lee, Oprah and even Nelson Mandela. They all had their own way of connecting with me at the time. I needed to hear their messages and, to be honest, they all were a part of my healing process in some way, shape or form.

With that in mind, my next goal was to contact three of the people who had guided me through their videos and somehow touch them with my art, as a way of saying thank you. So I wrote down specific names: Anthony Robbins, Deepak Chopra and Dr. Wayne Dyer. I had no plan for how I would reach these people, especially as they were all high-profile personalities and all lived overseas.

As in the past, I asked the universe to guide me and show me the right steps and procedures to land my art before the eyes of these three individuals on my list. I placed my request on my vision board, where I could see it daily but not be fixated on it, and let the angels do the rest.

I continued to perform at charity events and also ventured into product launches for various companies. I would research particular corporations I wanted to collaborate with, send a general email, then wait for responses. I probably sent about 30 emails out per day, mostly receiving *We will keep your details on file for future reference* in return.

Until one day I received an email response with the heading *IMPORTANT.* My eyes were naturally drawn to this particular email, which was a response from a company I'd emailed two months prior, with a collaboration request. It was from a major London-based fashion house that produced luxury loafer shoes. The email was sent by their Managing Director, and he was very interested.

I could not believe it. I immediately responded, requesting a Skype meeting and happily, they accepted. After a number of online meetings and detailed email exchanges, contracts were drawn up. The universe had once again confirmed that my journey and purpose had been found, and I needed to share it with the world.

I could now add to my name 'international shoe designer', as I had just signed a global contract to design my very own luxury loafer for men, to be available online from early 2015.

The first phase of my two major goals had been achieved with little effort. I was truly over the moon, and not only because I had just landed my first international art collaboration contract. I was also flowing with happiness, knowing that the universe had once again delivered to me what I needed, when I needed it, and I had learnt enough through the hard years to recognise the signs.

I was very excited to see how and when phase two would be achieved, as I had no idea how I would land my paintings in the hands of international speakers, teachers and world leaders. But that was the most exciting part, not knowing and just waiting for the signs, as I continued on with my daily passion and purpose.

Once the shoe design contracts were signed, I really had to start practising for my New Zealand performance, as 2015 was approaching. This would be my first one-hour direct audience talk, as well as my first in another country.

I had spoken at charity events in the past but they had not been long in duration and watered-down versions of my story to accompany my art performance. This time the stage was all mine. I now had the opportunity to speak about my story, my way, my truth, and explain to an audience who wanted to know about me how I'd gone from hospital bed to world stage.

As I started to write my talk, I found myself becoming a little stuck—writer's block if you will. The content was there, I just needed an eloquent way to deliver it to my audience. I decided to revert back to some of the teachings from the indirect mentors I had watched while in hospital.

Now with no real direction about who I would watch that day or why, I decided to go back and study Dr. Wayne Dyer. This is when things got interesting. If you research Dr. Wayne Dyer (or any of the personalities I have mentioned) on the internet, an abundance of information pops up, especially videos. In this case I wanted to watch a live video, one that featured a large audience, to study how Dr. Dyer delivered his message and how I could adapt my story accordingly. A number of videos popped up and I randomly clicked one; for some reason I had connection with it.

The video loaded and I turned away to grab my notepad and there it was, the title of the video. The universe had directed me once again. I was about to watch Dr. Wayne Dyer speak at an event online in front of a large crowd. The event was called *Wanderlust*, held in Squaw Valley in 2012.

I could not believe what I was seeing! I had randomly clicked on a video to research and study for my up-and-coming talk, and it happened to be a video from one of my indirect mentors who had helped me through my pain in hospital, talking at the same festival as I was booked for.

If there were any ounce of negativity, anxiety or fear, flowing through my body at that point, I can assure you it was erased immediately. It had been further confirmed that my journey was heading exactly in the direction it needed to.

I spoke at *Wanderlust New Zealand* in January 2015 to a room of approximately 100 people. I was a little nervous, but I could feel the crowd's energy, and I could see in their eyes they were there because they wanted to know my story. That day I spoke for just over an hour. I explained my journey up until that point, including the Dr. Wayne Dyer alignment, and even painted a portrait while I spoke. I wasn't sure how I was going to be received that day; all I knew was that the words I spoke were real, they were raw and from my heart. I left my soul on the canvas, so to speak.

I received my first standing ovation that day. I was held back for forty minutes after my talk as many shared their stories of health struggles, resulting in many hugs and happy tears of exchange. All left with a thank you for being the voice they needed to hear to help them on their journey.

I returned home from my first overseas performance and speaking engagement very satisfied with what I had achieved. I spent the next day at home with my family, sharing my experience and photos, leaving an angelic glow in the room.

The next day I checked my emails; I'd been out of range while I was away. I wasn't inundated with too many, but the few that were in there would once again change the course of my life's purpose and see me achieve phase two of my 'nothing is impossible' goals.

Prior to leaving for New Zealand, I sent a number of desires out into the universe. I had painted a portrait of Dr. Wayne Dyer, placed it on my website, and reached out to a few of his team including his family members, with a quick introductory email. The purpose of that was not to gain recognition; it was simply to pay homage to someone who had been an inspiration and had impact on my life. Painting his portrait was my way of saying thank you. If I ever had a chance to meet him, I would most definitely present him with his very own Matteo portrait.

I put the second law of attraction in place when I found out that Anthony Robbins was going to be speaking in Sydney in early 2015, at one of the most influential wealth-creation events. I sent an email to the Managing Director of the company hosting the event, with an outline of who I was, including the notion of opening for Anthony Robbins, prior to him walking on stage in Sydney. I'd sent that email off just before I left for New Zealand.

I'd also found out that Deepak Chopra was to be in Australia on a tour while I was away. So before leaving for New Zealand, I tracked down the company hosting his tour and sent them a portrait I had painted of Deepak, with a letter to the Managing Director outlining my story. I hoped they would present my gift to Deepak on my behalf.

While I was away, the universe was once again working its magic, to bring to life the three thoughts I had put into motion prior to leaving for New Zealand. I sat down to open my emails that day and there they were, one after the other. The first email was an email from the Managing Director of the company hosting Deepak Chopra's tour. It included an image of Deepak Chopra standing on stage, holding the painting I had created. The Managing Director thanked me and said Deepak thought I was very talented and wanted to express his gratitude.

I just sat there staring at the computer screen looking at one of the people who had helped me throughout my years of illness. There he was, holding a painting that I had created and, better still, he now knew who Matteo Charles was.

After seeing that email I was content. If I hadn't opened any more emails that day, I would have been more than happy that I had reached one person on my list. But when the universe speaks and your ears are ready to listen, the universe will sing!

There were probably another twenty unread emails, but only two had a priority sign and the headings were in capitals. The first was a Facebook message link, sent by the daughter of Dr. Wayne Dyer. I couldn't believe it. I opened the email and read that his daughter had included me on a Facebook post, so I immediately opened the link. It was the portrait I had painted of Dr. Wayne Dyer before I left for New Zealand, which I had posted on my website and social media channels. Dr. Wayne Dyer had reposted the painting on his Facebook page; he had quoted me from my website and personally thanked me for sharing my art with the world.

I stared again at the Facebook post. It had been posted by someone who had helped me through my darkest times and here I was, watching him personally thank me for sharing my art with the world.

What gave that story even further substance and will forever touch my heart was that almost one year later I had a private meeting with Dr. Wayne W. Dyer. I met him while he was on tour in Australia, during a short holiday in Sydney with his two daughters. I was privileged to meet the man who helped me through my dark days.

I presented him with a painting, I presented his daughters with their own paintings, and will never forget looking into Dr. Wayne Dyer's eyes, as he said in the kindest voice, 'Thank you, that is very kind of you.' It was as though the world had stopped and it was just him and me. I was deeply grateful beyond words for that moment.

Two weeks later, I learnt that Dr. Wayne Dyer had passed away and I was stopped in my tracks. I could not believe what I was hearing as I had been with him only two weeks before. Sadness surged through my soul, there were no words. I made my way to my studio and picked up the signed portrait I had painted for myself and had Dr. Dyer sign for me and started to cry. Then, all of a sudden, my tears stopped. I felt an abundance of gratitude, as I recognised the higher source had led me to meet Dr. Dyer in person only two weeks before he left this earth. This confirmed the journey I was on and that I needed to continue to share my story with the world and touch many lives, just as Dr. Dyer had done.

Now back to opening my emails ... I truly don't think I could have taken any more news from the positive realm at that time. It truly felt like all of my prayers had been answered at once. But I had one final important email to read, that would literally take me and my brand to a whole new level.

I thought I better open that final email before I had a happiness meltdown. I can remember thinking this final email could not be as huge as the past two. After all, I had just reached two people on my list who I wanted to thank; they had acknowledged my journey and passion and shared it with the world through their platforms.

The final email had an attachment. I thought it was another photo. As I clicked it open, my eyes almost popped out of their sockets. It was an email from the Managing Director of the promotional company that was bringing out Anthony Robbins. The email was brief but read along the lines of: *Matteo, I received your email, website, and watched your videos. I was taken aback by your work and feel it could be a great fit for our up-and-coming event. To save time, I have enclosed a performance contract for you. If you are in agreement, I would like you to come in, sign the papers and lock you in to open for Anthony Robbins.*

I had achieved what I'd set out to do. Not only had I reached the mentors who had taken me out of the trenches of my personal health war, I had shared with them my purpose and passion for art. Now I was about to open for one of the world's most influential speakers.

One week later, I signed contracts to open for Anthony Robbins. Three months later, I painted Anthony Robbins' portrait live in ten minutes, in front of 3000 people. I was able to meet him personally, have photos with him and present him with his very own Matteo painting. Six months later, the same company hired me to open in Sydney and Melbourne, Australia for one of the world's most recognisable and influential businessmen, Sir Richard Branson, that was truly a humbling experience.

On Novemeber 28th 2015 I was personally invited to perform in Hong Kong for the celebration of Bruce Lee's 75th Anniversary. Performing at a V.I.P private event, meeting Bruce Lee's Wife, Linda and Daughter Shannon. That evening elevated my attitude of gratitude and confirmed the continuous path I need to travel.

Those events elevated my brand to the next level; a level that I didn't know existed. With everything that had happened up until that point, my achievements and failures, something had always stood out. Something was always working behind the scenes, even if I couldn't see it at the time. The end result or, should I say the beginning of the beginning, illustrated to me that there would ultimately be art in greatness.

Chapter 16

The Final Masterpiece

Growing up, you don't really have control over many things. You don't control what you eat, as your parents or guardians put food literally on the table; you don't control which family you are born into; you don't control what race you are born into or run, not even where you live.

But as you grow older, your circumstances mould you into the person you are today and that can be a blessing in disguise. That blessing is something you don't realise has happened until you look in the mirror ... perhaps you're not happy with what's looking back or perhaps you're at total peace with yourself as a being.

Some of us find our dream job or our dream job finds us; some are lucky and find their spouse in high school and live that fairytale life with a happy ending. Some bounce from partner to partner, never really finding that true spark with one person. They may find a small spark in each person they have been with, hoping to find someone who possesses all of the best qualities from past relationships in one superhuman being.

Is there such a thing as a superhuman being? Are we all superhuman beings but, as we are conformed to live a certain way, we miss our own greatness? Can you imagine living in a world where everyone followed their dreams and passions? There would be no wars, no drugs, no poverty, no racism, no crime—just one big, colourful canvas of a world.

Well, I can dream of such a world. Perhaps not to the extent I just described, as there needs to be some order in the world. But following your dreams; ending poverty, crime and pain; increasing self-awareness of who we are; and taking control of our own lives where we can. That's my dream and what I live for today.

I was diagnosed with a non-curable disease at quite a young age, the first in my family to have such an illness. I knocked on heaven's, hell's and death's doors multiple times. I fought depression, anxiety and suicidal thoughts. I lost a fortune, I lost my businesses and, most importantly, I lost me as a person.

As I look into the souls of people listening to my story, I always begin by stating who I am and that a number of years ago I was blessed to be diagnosed with a non-curable disease. This often results in very curious reactions from my listeners. I continue to explain that I am blessed to have been diagnosed with a non-curable chronic disease because when I was admitted to hospital I entered with one set of eyes but came out with a brand-new set.

Having a disease that no-one can see makes life very difficult and, in turn, forces you to rethink your every action. I often say that if I cut myself with a knife, your physical eyes would see the blood pouring out and immediately you would feel sympathy for me. But having an internal disease that no-one can see makes life very difficult; there have been times when people, even my family and work associates, have not been able to associate with my pain and therefore sympathise with my situation.

Did I yearn for sympathy? No! Did I yearn for understanding? Yes! And that was something that was hard to come by.

I had to create a lifestyle of my own and self-employment seemed the only option. Many professional defeats had left a bad taste in my mouth, and the thought of dealing with my disease while working at yet another 'job' was not something I could easily entertain.

Finding a partner became a very minimal concern. Not many people today would put up with living with a disease if they had one themselves, let alone having to take care of someone who had one of their own from such a young age.

But the lessons I have learnt through my disease were more profound than I could have ever imagined. I would never have thought that being diagnosed with a non-curable chronic disease would be a new form of education. It proved to be the highest form of street knowledge from the University of Life that one could dream of. I learnt things indirectly so that certain habits are now ingrained in my professional and personal actions today.

I have had multiple career triumphs and defeats. I was abused, taken advantage of, and used as a punching bag. But for all that I still say thank you. Thank you for kicking me when I was down; thank you for testing my faith when I didn't believe in life and its true meaning; thank you for showing me who my true friends are and which family members really cared.

But most importantly, thank you for providing me with a handbook. A personalised handbook that was designed, constructed, experienced and then written by me, to be taught to those who are ready. A handbook that clearly outlines the path I needed to pave, or the seeds I needed to plant, in order for my personal Garden of Eden to sprout and flourish.

The information in this handbook is not of this world, it is priceless. It is something that can't be seen physically but I can see it clearly, each time I close my eyes. It is shown through my every daily action.

I have developed somewhat of a military mind, a forward-thinking, strategic mindset. My aim is to help and inspire others through my story, and to better my own life with periodic flashbacks.

How do I help? Well, in every area I can. Sometimes it is a direct action, when I cross paths with someone who I find to be a silent sufferer, as I was. Sometimes it is more indirect, as when I offer my story to inspire others.

I am very conscious of what I eat. Your insides reflect your feelings and emotions on the outside. If you put garbage in, you will be garbage. So the old saying: *You are what you eat* is something that I live by.

I exercise daily; not a lot, but I do what I love. There are a million and one programs on the market telling you to exercise this way, eat this and don't eat that. My suggestion is to find a form of exercise, no matter what it is, that you enjoy and do that. That way you will do more of it and, in turn, become healthier and fitter; it's a very easy formula.

I try to be very conscious of how I speak to people. Words are the most dangerous weapon of mass destruction in the world today; they have the power to both create and destroy. If you are careless with your words, in most cases they will destroy and it will be silent, slow and painful to the recipient.

I take time out for myself. I love business, all aspects of it, but there needs to be a work-life balance. If you work in sales, you will know the importance of setting up multiple appointments daily to sell your product and fill up your diary. Set up an appointment for you, you are just as important as your product and your clients. Believe me, I know that if you're lying in a hospital bed, no matter how much money you have it won't save you; and, if you have lived an immoral life, that's when it will hit you and it will be too late.

I am constantly hungry for knowledge. While technology is a distraction today, if you know how to harness it, knowledge is literally at our fingertips.

Having a disease forced me to place my mind in forward-thinking situations and that has filtered through into much of my work today. I used to plan my trips many hours in advance, my exact route including where the bathrooms would be, in case of a sudden bowel emergency. I used to carry my emergency bag containing underwear, tissues and wet wipes. I would always have something to clean myself with and change into, no matter how embarrassing it was.

Each time I use a public bathroom today, before I do anything else, I check that a toilet roll is available, as I have come unstuck so many times in the past. More often than not I wear a singlet under my T-shirt; that way if there is no toilet paper I could use that to wipe myself.

If I only need to urinate in a public toilet, I lift the seat up and leave it up. This is not because I'm a male, but because I know that males urinate all over the toilet seat in public toilets. I always think back to when I had to sit on other's urine, because I didn't have the time to wipe the seat down. I don't want anyone else to go through that added pain, so this is one of the ways I feel I can give back.

Most of the time I keep my arms shaved, while the rest of my body is quite hairy. I don't do this to be a metrosexual; it's force of habit. This stems from the first time I was admitted into hospital, when the doctors were rough taking needles out of me and ripping my hair out in the process.

All of these things may seem quite menial, but they are very important to me. They are a constant reminder of what I have learnt and enhance my forward-thinking abilities.

And what comes with a forward-thinking mindset? Well, you almost become a magician, you are able to see things others cannot. I am able to analyse more quickly and more accurately than most executives from top *Fortune 500* companies. But most importantly, it has opened my eyes and allowed me to find something within that seems to be lost in this time of technology. That is my common sense, which isn't so common anymore!

Every day I wake is a blessing. I am able to eat a meal without having to rush to the toilet; I am able to go out to dinner with loved ones and laugh without pain hitting me unexpectedly.

Hopefully, I have brought some peace to my parents' and brother's lives, knowing that I have come through the worst and they don't have to worry about my health anymore. My family is a family of worriers, as my brother always says: *Be a warrior, not a worrier.* So I don't think my parents will ever stop worrying, but I hope some ease has entered their life with the new chapter I am living.

I continue to conduct business. I have my fingers in many pies, so to speak, but always keep a conscious eye on what I am doing and why; whether what I am doing will hurt me or others, especially my family.

I control what enters my senses, my eyes, ears and mouth. I love to listen to ebooks in the car to further my education, as I have not even scratched the surface of the knowledge on offer today.

Don't get me wrong; I love my music and my entertainment past will always be a positive memory, so I still pump my favourite tunes every now and then on CD as I am driving. But that's exactly what it is—a CD—a form of music that I am in total control of.

I don't read newspapers, watch the news or read gossip magazines. They will not, and are not designed to, benefit me in any way. So I have no need for them. I have learnt that each and every person in this world is different. Most would see this as an obvious observation but if so, next time we have (say) a car accident or someone accidently bumps into us in the street we wouldn't be so quick to anger.

As for the thing that had temporarily taken over my body ... well, I don't say I am cured. 'Cured' is such a strong word and many people are prone to use things against you or watch you every day like a hawk, waiting for something to happen.

I live drug free. Most 'professionals' would say I am in remission and that is fine; they are allowed to say what they wish. But I am not in remission, I am in heaven. I am in heaven living a physical life that is limitless, and no-one will ever take that away from me.

The experiences I've had haven't all been pretty but the lessons have been priceless. The pain, well the pain was pain. Sometimes I handled it well and other times I didn't. (Like when the doctor inserted a needle into my wrist which felt like it was a metre long deep into my arm as it entered my artery, trying to extract blood to test my oxygen levels, and I could not breathe from the amount of blood I'd lost. That pain I didn't handle so well.)

As for the present moment, I am on a journey—a journey of wellness, a continuing journey of self-help. Many people will try and tell you what to do in your life; the keyword being 'your' life. Listen, but only inhale what is useful for you. Throw away the rest into the rubbish bin of life and never think about it again.

That's how I live. Do I want you to live like me, absolutely not! Why? Because you are an individual, a powerful source of energy, and you need to live for you. What has worked for me may not work for you, although in some areas it may. It is all a matter of trial and error until you find your equilibrium. We are all born to shine as ourselves, otherwise we would all be from a production line with the same computing system running the same software.

We have the ability to be whatever we want to be, that's the power of being human. A bird can only be a bird, a dog only a dog, but a human can be whatever it wants and change whenever it wants. That's a powerful ability to have, almost superhuman

If you, or someone you know, are suddenly diagnosed with something, don't let that take over your mind; don't allow emotion to overtake your intelligence. Do what I didn't do for a long time and research the cures. If they say there aren't any, make sure you find one and prove everyone wrong and yourself proud.

That's what I found to be most satisfying. Sure, it's nice to make our parents, family and loved ones proud but truly, who do we have to make proud? The only person in the world who has been there for you since the day you were born, has experienced everything you have, both positive and negative, and who will never leave your side ... You!!

Strive to make yourself proud because, when you do, it will illuminate the physical world and people will notice. When that happens, you will shine so brightly that, without knowing, you will light up every room you enter. People will have no choice but to be drawn to you, find out what you do, and be proud to have met you.

You can't please everyone and you never will. Quite frankly, why would you want to? There are billions of people in this world and if it was your mission to please them all, you would live a pretty boring, pointless and meaningless life.

You are the light, your own light, let your soul guide you. Be patient, things will happen when the time is right; ask and you shall receive. I asked. Hell, I begged, I pleaded, I screamed! And eventually my way was shown. But it wasn't when I wanted it to be shown, it was when the higher source wanted to show me.

When it happens you will know, as you will be ready. How do you know when you are ready? You won't. Things will happen and you will find yourself having strength you have never had before, doing things you have no training for, and completing the task at hand better than someone who studied for years to learn that particular skill. In that moment, when you stop and think about what you have just achieved, all that will enter your mind will be the still thoughts of nothing; that's when you will know.

My knowing comes and goes daily in various areas of my personal and working life. I pray and meditate daily, which helps me to keep my soul open to the non-physical world. I guess that strengthens my personal security blanket of knowing that the higher source (or God) is always working behind the scenes for me.

What does this knowing get you in life? Well I don't know, as I don't know what you want, only you do. Perhaps you don't and it will come to you. For me, the knowing has helped me to find and live my purpose through something that was always present for me since a young age in life—and that was my art.

My art has helped me and directed me to certain people who have enriched my life and deleted others that pollute it. It has allowed me to see things before they happen and watch them sprout into fruition.

Don't be afraid of that word 'fear', as that's exactly what it is—a word. A bunch of lines scribbled in books or on a piece of paper designed to hold us back. But if you truly think about it, fear is just another 'thing' that humans have created to inflict conformity into our lives. If you break it down to its core, fear itself is not real; it has no arms or legs, not even a mouth to physically or verbally abuse us. So when inflicted on us the word 'fear', just like 'failure', only has an effect if we allow it to. That's right, only if we allow it to!

I have lived in fear for many years because I knew no better. I lived in fear of leaving the house, in case I needed to suddenly use the bathroom. I was afraid to venture into businesses I knew little about; I was afraid to fail, because of the impact that would have on my bank account. Most importantly, I was in fear of finding my true self and true purpose in life.

But that's not why we are born. We are supposed to try, fail, learn and sometimes be afraid. It's when those conformed words of mass destruction are heading our way that we put on our best armour and fight, not in a literal way, but for our morals and personal standards of living. Don't allow anyone to convince you otherwise.

Today I have cracked the code of inspiration and share it with the world daily. I am able to utilise my passion for art and writing, combined with my story, to help inspire and bring out the silent sufferers of this world, whether it be one-on-one or in front of a crowd of thousands.

I took the biggest leap of faith and faced fear and failure head on. I proved to the conformed society that, no matter where you are born or your circumstances, if you truly are willing to see the light, you will have no choice but to paint for the world the message that will truly be your final masterpiece.

My Empty Canvas

An empty canvas is where I bleed,
My soul speaks its truth and every need,
Each brushstroke I take,
Barer I'm stripped,
My heart is broken but mainly ripped,
I continue to paint hoping the pain will cease,
Unbeknown to me,
Will I ever finish this masterpiece?

Your Shift

When you shift,
You have your gift,
A gift from above,
Sent with love,
Full of abundance
You are no more redundant,
Peace and love,
This is your dove,
High as a kite,
Your world shines so bright,
Heaven on earth,
This is now your rebirth,
Health is wealth,
You have finally found yourself.

The Universe

The universe provides enough evidence for your
soul to continue on your purpose,
To reach a level of living in abundance.

Inspiration

Inspiration is the spirit's elevation to freedom,
Freedom from the daily grind,
Daily forcing us to run and hide,
Inspiration allows us to be free and wild,
And continue to live as a child,
Innocent and free,
Embracing what we are truly meant to be,
One with the earth,
One with our spirit,
One with the source,
Continuing on life's journey,
To discover our true purpose and course.

What Is Life?

(Written by a being becoming human)
What is life when everything we are, everything we do and everything we
use, in the end is disposable and replaceable? What is life when we value
things that don't breathe, things without a soul? Yet what breathes and has
a soul we take advantage of, and are quick to hurt with words or violence.
Have we become something that doesn't have the right to be called
human anymore? Our respect exists no more, our selfishness has
only grown stronger, living for ourselves and not others.
What is life when family become strangers? When there
is enough wealth to share, yet most are bare?
What is life when a pair of shoes become higher in
value than one's moral code and views?

Has life become a 'thing'? Where did we go wrong?
Is it evil? Are we evil? What is evil?
To live in a world, to create a life, is a privilege that
most will only experience through a dream.
Dreams are life, perhaps of this world, maybe the next, maybe already lived.
Either way, what is life when the difference between reality, greed
and our dreams cannot be deciphered through common sense?
To me, life can only be living in forever's eternity, whatever that may be.

Free

When I close my eyes brushstrokes appear,
What the world doesn't know is I paint from fear,
Paint splats fill the room with no direction in mind,
Colour and sight not leaving me blind,
Which way will fear direct me?
Each stroke I take, the room brightens with light,
I feel at ease knowing everything will be alright,
My canvas is complete staring back at me,
All along allowing me to be wild and free.

instagram@matteocharles
Facebook/matteocharlesart
Youtube Matteo Charles
www.matteocharles.com

Printed in the United States
By Bookmasters